Pocket Guide to Chicago Architecture

Judith Paine McBrien

Illustrations by John F. DeSalvo

W. W. Norton & Company
New York • London

To Vincent W. McBrien

A NORTON PROFESSIONAL BOOK
Copyright © 1997 by Judith Paine McBrien
Copyright © 1993, 1992, 1991 by Perspectives International, Inc.

For information about permission to reproduce selections from this book, write to
Permissions, W. W. Norton & Company, Inc., 500 Fifth Avenue, New York NY 10110.

The text of this book is composed in 10 point Gill Sans
with the display set in 16 point Gill Sans Bold
Composition and book design by Karen Dangremond
Manufacturing by Haddon Craftsmen

Library of Congress Cataloging-in-Publication Data

McBrien, Judith Paine.
    Pocket guide to Chicago architecture / Judith Paine McBrien ; illustrations by
John F. DeSalvo.
        p. cm.
    "A Norton professional book."
    Includes index.
    ISBN 0-393-73013-1 (pbk.)
    I. Architecture—Illinois—Chicago—Guidebooks. 2. Chicago (Ill.)—Buildings,
structures, etc.—Guidebooks. I. Title.
    NA735.C4M42 1996
    720'.9773'11—dc20   96-38750
                                                CIP

ISBN 0-393-73013-1 (pbk.)

W. W. Norton & Company, Inc., 500 Fifth Avenue, New York N.Y. 10110
        http://www.wwnorton.com

W. W. Norton & Company Ltd., 10 Coptic Street, London WC1A 1PU

0 9 8 7 6 5 4 3

Contents

Introduction

Chicago is often described as a city of neighborhoods because of the size, diversity, and strength of the ethnic groups who call it home. Chicago's downtown, too, is composed of neighborhoods: Michigan Avenue, the Loop, and the Riverfront.

Michigan Avenue is Chicago's Main Street and cultural core. South of the Chicago River, it borders Grant Park, a grand civic lawn sweeping to Lake Michigan beyond. Facing the park is the famous cliff of Michigan Avenue structures, separate yet related, like members of an extended family. At the corners of the Michigan Avenue Bridge are some of Chicago's most beloved buildings: 333 North Michigan Avenue, the London Guarantee & Accident Building, the Wrigley Building and the Chicago Tribune Tower. North Michigan Avenue was conceived as an elegant boulevard and its development in the 1920s was stylistically eclectic. Today it includes large mixed use towers, such as the John Hancock Center, as well as what is perhaps Chicago's most historic symbol, the Water Tower that survived the great 1871 fire.

Historically, the Loop is Chicago's commercial neighborhood. The business district was small and intensely developed because it was hemmed in on four sides: by the Chicago River on the west and north, Lake Michigan on the east, and massive railroad yards on the south. This physical constraint combined with the urgency to rebuild after the 1871 fire, and the availability of new inventions and technologies and a willingness to use them, led to the Loop's renown as the birthplace of the skyscraper. Today one can walk across the Loop in fifteen minutes and see the development of modern architecture from the earliest high rises to the Sears Tower. It is a remarkable journey, one on which Chicago's reputation for innovative engineering and design can best be experienced.

Chicago began on the banks of the Chicago River where it met Lake Michigan. In the mid-nineteenth century, the river was teeming with ships transporting such bountiful supplies of grain, lumber, and coal that Chicago became one of the largest ports in the world. As the railroads developed, the city turned its back on the river, and it became a polluted waterway lined with industrial warehouses. Today the Chicago River has been revitalized into a clean blue waterway offering magnificent view corridors that attract high-rise developments. Thus, Chicago's riverfront is an area where the past meets the present in a particularly compelling way.

Whether you are exploring on foot or by boat, this guide is an introduction to Chicago's important contributions to modern urban design. It is divided into three sections, each of which offers a concentrated tour of the downtown neighborhoods. Proud of its building tradition, Chicago invites you to discover its architecture, bridges, and parks.

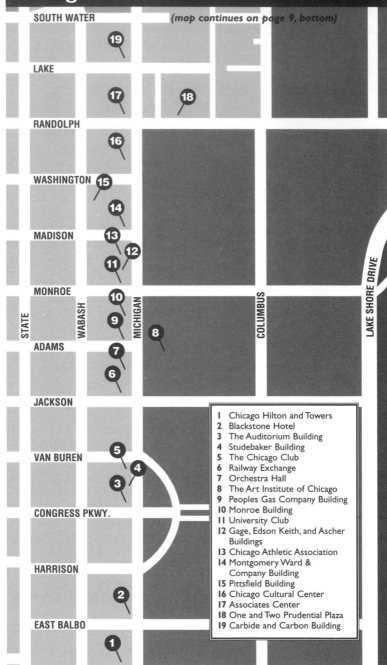

Michigan Avenue

(map continues on page 9, bottom)

SOUTH WATER

LAKE

RANDOLPH

WASHINGTON

MADISON

MONROE

ADAMS

JACKSON

VAN BUREN

CONGRESS PKWY.

HARRISON

EAST BALBO

STATE

WABASH

MICHIGAN

COLUMBUS

LAKE SHORE DRIVE

1   Chicago Hilton and Towers
2   Blackstone Hotel
3   The Auditorium Building
4   Studebaker Building
5   The Chicago Club
6   Railway Exchange
7   Orchestra Hall
8   The Art Institute of Chicago
9   Peoples Gas Company Building
10 Monroe Building
11 University Club
12 Gage, Edson Keith, and Ascher
    Buildings
13 Chicago Athletic Association
14 Montgomery Ward &
    Company Building
15 Pittsfield Building
16 Chicago Cultural Center
17 Associates Center
18 One and Two Prudential Plaza
19 Carbide and Carbon Building

8

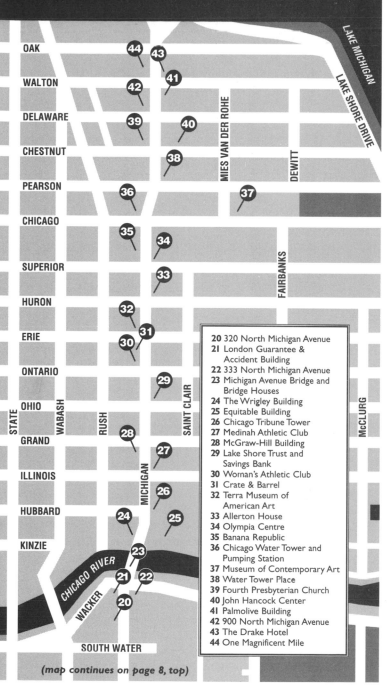

OAK

WALTON

DELAWARE

CHESTNUT

PEARSON

CHICAGO

SUPERIOR

HURON

ERIE

ONTARIO

OHIO

GRAND

ILLINOIS

HUBBARD

KINZIE

STATE
WABASH
RUSH
MICHIGAN
SAINT CLAIR
MIES VAN DER ROHE
DEWITT
FAIRBANKS
McCLURG

LAKE MICHIGAN

LAKE SHORE DRIVE

CHICAGO RIVER

WACKER

SOUTH WATER

20 320 North Michigan Avenue
21 London Guarantee & Accident Building
22 333 North Michigan Avenue
23 Michigan Avenue Bridge and Bridge Houses
24 The Wrigley Building
25 Equitable Building
26 Chicago Tribune Tower
27 Medinah Athletic Club
28 McGraw-Hill Building
29 Lake Shore Trust and Savings Bank
30 Woman's Athletic Club
31 Crate & Barrel
32 Terra Museum of American Art
33 Allerton House
34 Olympia Centre
35 Banana Republic
36 Chicago Water Tower and Pumping Station
37 Museum of Contemporary Art
38 Water Tower Place
39 Fourth Presbyterian Church
40 John Hancock Center
41 Palmolive Building
42 900 North Michigan Avenue
43 The Drake Hotel
44 One Magnificent Mile

(map continues on page 8, top)

Holabird and Roche
700–46 South Michigan Avenue
1925–7
Renovation: Solomon Cordwell Buenz and Associates (architects) with Hirsch/Bedner and Associates (interior designers), 1986
Formerly Stevens Hotel

When this massive, 25-story hotel was completed in the Roaring Twenties, it was the largest in the world, with 3,000 guest rooms, an eighteen-hole rooftop golf course, and its own hospital. The hotel also aspired to be the most elegant, and hence looked to French classical and rococo styles for inspiration. The exterior is grand but subdued. A base and top of Bedford limestone frame the red brick central section, where three large light wells divide the mass into four vertical sections. Inside, however, is all Louis XVI luxe. The Grand Ballroom was modeled after the Palace of Versailles: washed in pinks, cream, and powder blue, it features 24-carat gold leaf and crystal chandeliers and a series of golden arched doorways linked by gilt-framed pastoral murals. The double-story Grand Stair Hall, with marble pilasters and a ceiling of painted clouds, continues the theme. Though the hotel's opening met with rave reviews, hotelier James W. Stevens (1853–1936) was able to enjoy the enterprise only briefly. By 1932, the hotel was in receivership, a victim of the Great Depression; four years later it was bankrupt. Fortunately, a recent renovation has restored its splendid spaces.

Marshall and Fox
630 South Michigan Avenue
1908

The Blackstone was the first high-rise hotel built on Michigan Avenue. Its French Second Empire style represented the ultimate in elegant taste; its creators represented the best of Chicago society. It was developed by John B. (1872–1964) and Tracy C. (1864–1939) Drake, sons of Chicago's noted hotelier John Burroughs Drake; the site was the former home of Timothy Blackstone, a family friend of the Drakes and president of the Chicago and Alton Railroad. When, after the 1871 Chicago Fire, other property types began to replace the fashionable rowhouses that had lined South Michigan Avenue, the pedigreed Blackstone became the hub of Chicago high society activity, accommodating the balls and debutante parties that families had formerly hosted in their homes. Creamy terra cotta is used above the pink granite foundation and again, shaded blue and green-gray, on the upper stories. Twelve stories of dark red brick rise from the base, with windows framed in slightly projecting terra-cotta architraves. These are capped by an ornamented mansard roof that once dominated the lakefront skyline. In 1910, architects Marshall and Fox designed the five-story granite Blackstone Theater on Balbo Street adjacent to the Blackstone Hotel.

Adler & Sullivan
430 South Michigan Avenue
1887–9

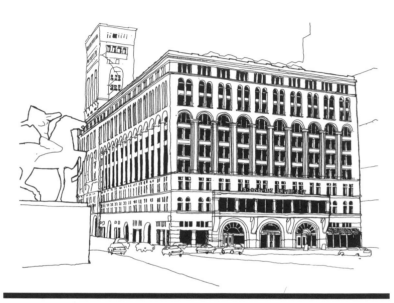

In 1886, Ferdinand Peck, a wealthy young businessman, organized the Chicago Auditorium Association to build a grand cultural and civic center befitting the brash, prosperous city of Chicago. He hired the firm of Adler & Sullivan, a small firm best known for their theater designs, to undertake the monumental multi-use project. They began with a simple, sturdy exterior, featuring a two-story, rough-hewn granite base topped by a floor of rusticated limestone, and above, smooth-faced limestone that created a flat wall plane from the fourth floor to the tower. A 400-room hotel is signaled by three great entrance arches on Michigan Avenue; office space was placed on Wabash Avenue and in the tower. Revenues from these spaces were to fund the heart of the structure: the Auditorium Theater. Here, Louis Sullivan displayed his brilliant designs combining naturalistic and geometric forms. Note how the new electrical illumination becomes an integral part of the composition. Unparalleled acoustics and sight lines were achieved in part by Dankmar Adler's use of a steeply raked auditorium floor and the manipulation of the interior plaster surfaces, including the great arches opening out from the stage. Since 1946, the Auditorium Building has been home to Roosevelt University.

Solon S. Beman
410 South Michigan Avenue
1885; renovation, 1898
Now known as the Fine Arts Building

This eleven-story building was designed by Solon S. Beman (1853–1914) with a Romanesque facade of rough-faced Bedford limestone and granite, and round-arched entries repeated in the upper floors. The Studebaker Building was originally built as a showroom for the Studebaker Carriage Company; carriages were displayed on the first four floors, which have the unusually large windows. Wagons were assembled upstairs. The roofline had a distinct silhouette, with two pyramids and three domes topping the five main bays. When the business moved to larger quarters, Beman was hired to convert the structure to use for artists, writers, and musicians. Two music halls and storefront shops replaced the ground-floor showrooms. The domes, the attic, and the original facade of the eighth floor were removed and replaced with a three-story addition. Renamed the Fine Arts Building in 1898, it contained 65 music studios, offices, and large tenant-artist quarters. Among the tenants were sculptor Lorado Taft; artist William W. Denslow, who drew illustrations for *The Wonderful Wizard of Oz* here; editors of *The Dial* literary magazine; the Municipal Art League; and on the ground floor, Browne's Bookstore, designed by Frank Lloyd Wright, who briefly rented space on the prestigious tenth floor.

Granger and Bollenbacher
81 East Van Buren Street
1930

The twelve-story Chicago Club, constructed of Connecticut brown-stone, shares its famous Michigan Avenue block with the Auditorium and Fine Arts buildings. It is an exemplum of contextuality, built long before "contextuality" became a Postmodern mantra, harmonizing with its neighbors in terms of scale, materials, proportion, and detail. Most notable are the block's recurrent two-story rusticated bases, variations in arched windows, and flat roofs. Here, the facade's surface is unornamented; the windows provide an interplay of solid and void that gives the mass a static poise. Burnham and Root's Art Institute (1887) stood on this site and was bought by the Chicago Club in 1893 when the Art Institute moved across the street (see #8). When the older building collapsed during a renovation in 1929, a new building was planned. Note the triple-arched entrance on Van Buren Street, which is a remnant of its distinguished predecessor. The architect, Alfred Hoyt Granger (1867–1939), was active in Chicago civic affairs and was the lone architect on the jury of the famed Chicago Tribune competition in 1922. His Chicago Club, founded in 1869, is among the city's most prestigious enclaves, many of which are located on Michigan Avenue.

D. H. Burnham and Co.
224 South Michigan Avenue
1903–4
Now known by its address

The seventeen-story Railway Exchange, later known as the Santa Fe Building, is one of D. H. Burnham and Co.'s most successful designs. The firm was a major stockholder in the building, and located its offices on the fourteenth floor. Like the firm's earlier Rookery building (1888), the Railway Exchange has a two-story open court, here made square and symmetrical; its mezzanine level is reached by a grand staircase. Above this, the 60- by 70-foot light well is faced in white enameled brick. The exterior walls are faced in a similarly pale cream, enameled terra cotta, and alternate flush and projecting bays in the main section, with flat surfaces at the building's base and top. Bull's-eye windows below the cornice function as both an additional light source and a decorative feature. Other classical motifs include Greek fretwork on the spandrels, antefixae at the cornice, and classical urns at the doorways. Consistent use of white brick and terra cotta recalled the White City of the 1893 Columbian Exposition; it also brightened the environment of Chicago's smoky, railroad-dominated downtown. Enameled terra cotta had a further advantage: city soot could simply be washed off.

D. H. Burnham and Co.
220 South Michigan Avenue
1904

This Neo-Georgian building illustrates the popularity of historic revivalism at the turn of the century. The corners are marked by quoins, which are topped by decorative swags just below the original cornice. The main four-story section of the building features regularly spaced double-hung windows against a flat brick surface, terminating in a limestone attic. This symmetrical facade highlights three tall, arched windows flanked by pedimented balcony doors on the second floor, behind which is the ballroom. The four-story auditorium is at the rear. The Cliff Dwellers Club, now moved, was added as a ninth floor in 1908, designed by architect Howard Van Doren Shaw (1869–1926). It is where member Louis Sullivan wrote *The Autobiography of an Idea*. The names of leading composers are incised on the frieze above the second-floor balcony; note also that of Theodore Thomas, below Bach. Thomas was the Chicago Symphony Orchestra's founder and first conductor. Incensed by empty concert seats in the too-large Auditorium Theater (see #3), he demanded the construction of this smaller space on threat of resignation. CSO trustee Daniel Burnham donated his services, and Thomas conducted the first concert here in 1904. Three weeks later he died.

Shepley, Rutan and Coolidge
Michigan Avenue at Adams Street
1892–3

Additions: McKinlock Court, Coolidge and Hodgdon, 1924; Ferguson Building, Holabird and Root, 1958; Morton Wing, Shaw, Metz and Associates, 1962; Rubloff Building, Skidmore, Owings & Merrill, 1976; Reconstruction of Stock Exchange Trading Room, Vinci/Kenny, 1977; Rice Building, Hammond, Beeby and Babka, 1988

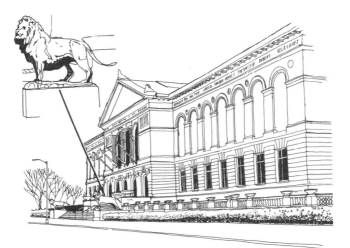

Built in conjunction with the World's Columbian Exposition of 1893, which used it for scholarly forums, the limestone Art Institute of Chicago was designed in the Beaux Arts style so prevalent at the Fair. Its symmetrical massing and classical decorative elements create a dignified exterior. The first-story walls are of rusticated limestone; the second, taller story has a smooth ashlar finish punctuated by a series of sculpture arcades and capped by a frieze reproducing the Parthenon's Panathenaic procession. Note the artists' names inscribed on the architrave. Interior spaces are organized in corridors off a grand central staircase. Established in 1879 as the Academy of Fine Arts, the museum grew quickly; by 1893, it had replaced W. W. Boyington's 1873 Inter-State Exposition Building in Lakefront (now Grant) Park. Sculptor Edward Kemeys (1843–1907) is responsible for the famous lions, symbols of strength and majesty, which have flanked the entrance since 1894. Over the past century, many additions have been constructed; the museum and its School now straddle the railroad tracks that once bounded the museum's east facade. Gardens on the south, designed by landscape architect Dan Kiley, and on the north by Hanna/Olin, are important components of the museum's design tradition.

D. H. Burnham and Co.
122 South Michigan Avenue
1911

The 22-story Peoples Gas Building stands on the site of Burnham and Root's Brunswick Hotel (1883), which in turn replaced the elegant H. H. Honoré family home, where Bertha Honoré married Potter Palmer. Huge granite columns march across the base of the building, but the weight of the exterior walls is actually carried on cantilevered girders at the second floor line. Like the nearby Railway Exchange building (see #6), also by D. H. Burnham and Co., a central light court opens above the third floor. The facade is divided into three parts: a columnar base, a textured shaft with pairs of regularly spaced double-hung windows, and from the seventeenth to twentieth floors, a colonnade made to look like granite, which is terra cotta instead. The corners are marked by flat piers, also of terra cotta. Originally, customer service was located in the central light court, in a room surrounded by two tiers of marble columns and topped by a Tiffany glass ceiling. Corporate pride extended to the building's private spaces, where state-of-the-art amenities included lavatories for every office suite, pneumatic cleaning equipment, and a public stenographer's office.

Holabird and Roche
104 South Michigan Avenue
1912

Designed in the Italian Gothic style, the sixteen-story Monroe Building was built to harmonize with the newly completed University Club on the opposite corner, also by Holabird and Roche (see #11). For example, its flat roof was changed to a gabled peak to repeat the University Club's silhouette, and its ornamental language is similarly historic. Above the twelfth story, the gable is emphasized by bifora windows that are smaller at the sides, and culminate in a double-storied window at the peak. Its first two stories, used for retail shops, are of pink-gray granite; the color scheme is continued above in matching terra cotta. The interior is equally remarkable: hallway and vestibules are of Rookwood tile, which is also used for the floors and wainscoting of the upper corridors of the building. Rookwood tile was popular during the Arts and Crafts movement in America and is characterized by the use of pastels and subtle glazing. The property was developed by Shepherd Brooks of Boston, who, with his brother Peter (1831–1920), developed many of Chicago's best-known buildings after the 1871 Chicago Fire, including the Monadnock, Marquette, and Pontiac buildings.

Holabird and Roche
26 East Monroe
1908–9

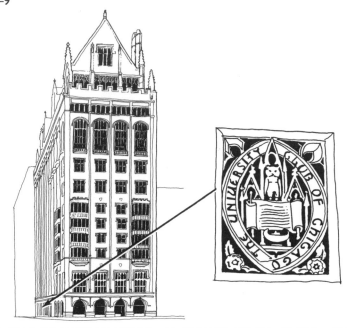

The University Club was formed in 1887 by a group of college graduates whose purpose was "the promotion of literature and art, by establishing and maintaining a library, reading room, and gallery of art." After twenty years of meeting in various quarters downtown, the association planned a building of its own. The twelve-story University Club rises at the corner of Monroe Street and Michigan Avenue on a steel skeletal frame, the same structural system used a decade earlier by the same architects for the neighboring Gage Group (see #12). But while those buildings express their internal cage, the University Club dresses its frame in Gothic robes and ornamentation, a style considered appropriate to its academic ties. This dignified, symmetrical facade cloaks a variety of functions: athletic facilities, meeting rooms, restaurants, a library, and rooms for overnight accommodations. On the second floor, the Michigan Room combines paneling and wood carving by architect Martin Roche with 56 ceiling panel paintings by club member Frederic Clay Bartlett (1873–1953), a noted art collector who donated Seurat's *Sunday Afternoon on the Island of Grand Jatte* to the Art Institute. Bartlett also designed the fourteen stained-glass windows in the three-story Cathedral Hall on the ninth floor.

Holabird and Roche
18, 24–28, and 30 South Michigan Avenue
1898–9
Now known as the Gage Group

In 1899, the Ascher, Edson Keith, and Gage companies, millinery wholesalers, relocated from quarters on Wabash Avenue to this new complex, which allowed each firm its own building and the greater natural light offered by lakefront exposure. These buildings, now known collectively as the Gage Group, have undergone several alterations and additions, but they remain a striking example of how an underlying steel structure can be expressed simply and directly on the exterior. The Ascher and Keith facades consist of unornamented brick and terra-cotta horizontal spandrels and vertical piers, creating a series of spaces filled by large, light-maximizing Chicago style windows, in which the fixed pane is flanked by a movable sash at each side. The taller Gage Building has an identical frame, but distinguishes itself with a facade designed by Louis Sullivan (1856–1924). The cream terra-cotta tile is decorated by two exuberant foliate forms exploding atop the piers and by smaller decorative forms repeated on the spandrels. The windows are composed of four casements below a band of Luxfer glass; the prismatic qualities of Luxfer glass created greater light diffusion, a recurrent concern in these designs and elsewhere before the widespread use of artificial light.

Henry Ives Cobb
12 South Michigan Avenue
1893

This eleven-story Venetian fantasy adds variety and interest to the wall of the buildings along Michigan Avenue. When completed, it boasted of having the largest number of athletic facilities under one roof, and it remains a private club today. The top two floors contain a great dining hall. Architect Henry Ives Cobb (1859–1931) was comfortable working in a variety of architectural styles, including Richardson Romanesque for the Newberry Library and former Chicago Historical Society, both 1892, as well as English Gothic for the first buildings of the University of Chicago. Among his best known designs was Potter Palmer's "castle" mansion on Lake Shore Drive (1882), which he designed in partnership with Charles Sumner Frost. In this clubhouse, he uses narrow lancet windows and tracery as decorative devices, and animates the facade with delicate brickwork. Note the frieze just below the cornice line; it features whimsical paired racquets in relief. Club architecture offered creative possibilities for design, as can be seen in other buildings on Michigan Avenue, such as the former Medinah Athletic Club (see #27), the University Club (see #11), and the Woman's Athletic Club (see # 30).

Richard C. Schmidt
6 North Michigan Avenue
1897–9
Addition: Holabird and Roche
c. 1923
Now known as
the Tower Building

Once the headquarters for the Montgomery Ward & Company, founded in 1872, this brick and terra-cotta building was for many years the dominant tower on Michigan Avenue. Located at the corner of Madison Street, it also marks the southern edge of Chicago's original grid: North Michigan Avenue officially begins here. Ward's mail-order business rapidly expanded along the block from its first location on the corner of Michigan Avenue and Washington Street, and finally a large new headquarters was commissioned. Containing warehouse distribution, marketing, and administrative functions under one roof, the building was nicknamed the "Busy Bee-Hive." Above a twelve-story base, a distinctive ten-story tower was topped by a famous gilded, electrically lit nude weathervane, *Progress Lighting the Way for Commerce*. The Montgomery Ward Building established the reputation of Richard C. Schmidt (1865–1959), who worked in association with Hugh M. G. Garden (1873–1961), later his partner. Numerous alterations to this building, including the demolition of the top five stories of the tower, have left it sadly disfigured. In 1908, the company relocated, for better transportation access and more space, to a new facility along the Chicago River designed by Schmidt, Garden and Martin.

Graham, Anderson, Probst and White
55 East Washington Street
1927

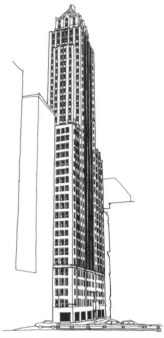

With its copper-roofed tower, the highest in the city when completed, the 38-story Pittsfield Building is a striking landmark just west of Michigan Avenue. It was developed by the Field estate in 1926. In 1922, the City of Chicago raised the height restriction on buildings to 264 feet, provided that the tower did not exceed one-quarter of the building's footprint or one-sixth its volume. Setbacks of one foot in ten from all sides of the adjacent property were also required. This 557-foot-tall skyscraper fulfilled these requirements with setbacks at the twenty-second, thirty-fifth, and thirty-eighth floors, which were emphasized with Gothic turrets. The polished black granite base, however, anticipates the Art Deco style, marking this building as a transitional one. The marriage of this most distinguished Chicago architectural firm and most prominent Chicago family would foster a continued evolution toward the modern aesthetic, in which massing dominates surface detail, as seen in the Field Building at 135 South LaSalle Street (1934). Although the offices in the Pittsfield Building were planned for medical tenants and related professionals, the building's five-story interior atrium uses rich marbles and brass details to create an elegant retail statement. Don't miss the elevator cabs and lobby mailbox.

Shepley, Rutan and Coolidge
78 East Washington Street
1897
Formerly Chicago Public Library

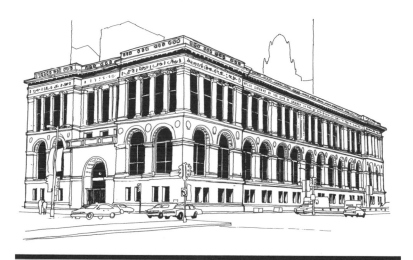

A restrained Italian Renaissance design, this four-story building of Bedford limestone and granite was the first permanent home of the Chicago Public Library, which began in 1871 as a depository for books donated by Great Britain after the Great Fire. It was built on the site of Dearborn Park and relates to the nearby Art Institute (see #8), also by Shepley, Rutan and Coolidge, in its low-scale, symmetrical form, use of repeating arches, and classical ornamental language. The interior includes remarkable mosaics from the House of Tiffany, executed by J. A. Holzer, including rotundas at the north and south with domes of Tiffany glass. The principal entrance is on Washington Street, where a grand staircase of white Carrara marble leads upward along mosaic-inlaid balustrades. On the Randolph Street side, a staircase leads to the Grand Army of the Republic Memorial Hall on the second floor. The Library Board included this hall in order to utilize the entire Dearborn Park site, part of which had been previously granted to a Civil War veterans group by the Illinois legislature. After Chicago's new library was completed in 1991, this building became Chicago's Cultural Center, which sponsors events and exhibitions for the community.

A. Epstein & Sons
150 North Michigan Avenue
1983–4

Now known as the
Stone Container Building

Overwhelming from street level, this speculative office building rends the fabric of Michigan Avenue by violating that which makes the buildings of the boulevard extraordinary—scale, siting, materials, proportion, and pedestrian amenities. The fourteen-story, masonry-clad John Crerar Library (1920) by Holabird and Roche was demolished for this structure. Its 41-story height dwarfs the Beaux Arts Cultural Center to the south; more important, it lacks the one- or two-story bases that connect the disparate buildings of this boulevard and relate them, regardless of size, to human scale. Instead of stone, brick, or terra cotta, its facade is horizontal aluminum banding, which has the effect of pulling the building out at the sides instead of soaring tall. It is placed on a 45-degree angle to the street, breaking the wall formed by the flush orientation of buildings on the edge of the grid facing the lakefront. Addressing Grant Park on a diagonal, its roofline sliced into two triangular towers, it stands thick and insistent on one of Chicago's most visible corners. It is best seen at night, when white lights outline the diamond-shaped roofline against the darkness.

138 East Randolph Street
Naess and Murphy
1952–5
Addition: C.F. Murphy and Associates, 1968
180 North Stetson Avenue
Loebl Schlossman and Hackl
1990

THE PRUDENTIAL
INSURANCE COMPANY OF AMERICA

This complex is located on a 3.3-acre site over the Illinois Central rail-yards, which stretch across 80 acres from Randolph Street north to the Chicago River and east to Lake Michigan. The 41-story One Prudential Plaza was the first skyscraper built after World War II in Chicago, replacing Holabird and Root's Board of Trade (1930) as the tallest building in the city. When completed in 1955, its flat-topped Indiana limestone slab with the company's name in red neon letters became a highly visible addition to the city's skyline. On the south facade between the eighth and eleventh floors, note the Rock of Gibraltar sculptural relief by Alfonso Ianelli (1889–1965), best known for his work on Frank Lloyd Wright's Midway Gardens. Thirty-five years later, Two Prudential Plaza was completed, designed by Loebl, Schlossman, Dart and Hackl, architects of Water Tower Place (see #38). Built of gray granite, to harmonize with the earlier building, and silver glass, this 64-story skyscraper is a sleek tower culminating in a multi-faceted peak and spire, reminiscent of New York's Chrysler Building. The two buildings share a common lobby level and are connected by two five-story atria.

Burnham Brothers
230 North Michigan Avenue
1929

This 40-story skyscraper is characterized by a series of setbacks that reflect the 1922 zoning ordinance aimed at providing more light at street level. What distinguishes the Carbide and Carbon Building among the monochromatic high-rises of Chicago is its coloring: polished black granite at the base, with shades of dark-green mottled terra cotta on floors four through twenty-six. Gold terra cotta accents the piers and pilasters at the top of the building, and marks the flower medallions at the top of the black granite base. Note too the swirling grillwork at the entrance. This decorative language is carried into the lobby, which has a gray Tennessee marble floor with a Belgian black marble border and bronze metalwork above the entrance, on elevators, and fixtures. Daniel (1886–1961) and Hubert (1882–1969) Burnham were sons of noted Chicago architect and planner Daniel Hudson Burnham; they designed several commercial buildings and hotels in the city, including the Bankers Building and the Seneca Hotel, both 1927. The building's form was inspired by the shape of a champagne bottle, so the story goes. True or not, its sparkling top and telescoping mass provide an exuberant reminder of Chicago in the boisterous, carefree Twenties.

Booth Hansen & Associates
1983

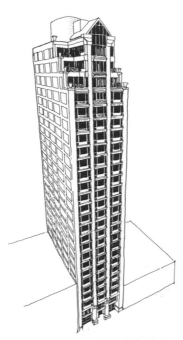

Built on a narrow 48-foot-wide lot, this 26-story, mixed-use project includes two levels of below-grade parking, retail space on the ground floor, offices on floors two through thirteen and residential condominiums above. Its continuous piers separate the exterior into three bays and carry the eye upward, culminating in splayed capitals intersected by a glass gabled penthouse. Setbacks on the top three stories allow for terraces that add interest to the facade and create spectacular views for the tenants. Architect Laurence Booth (b. 1936) used wide Chicago windows to create a regular rhythm on the facade. At the base, he fashioned double-story columns with an ogee curve that hides imperfections and water stains in the poured concrete, an imaginative solution to a budgetary constraint. Blank side walls of pink stucco assume future adjacent construction, but meanwhile, windows have been punched in for additional light and views. Trained at Harvard and the Massachusetts Institute of Technology and winner of numerous local and national design awards, Booth has designed apartments, residences, and adaptive reuse projects, including the nearby Terra Museum of American Art (see #32). Here he has created a slender, understated structure that adds dignity to the historic boulevard.

Alfred S. Alschuler
360 North Michigan Avenue
1922–3

As the Wrigley Building (see #24) was nearing completion, Alfred Alschuler (1876–1940) received a plum commission: the headquarters building for the London Guarantee & Accident Company, which would occupy the prominent site just across the Chicago River at the termination of Wacker Drive with the new Michigan Avenue Bridge. Alschuler was known primarily for his industrial work, although he also designed the terra-cotta Thompson Building (1912) at 350 North Clark Street, the K. A. M. Isaiah-Israel Synagogue in Chicago's Kenwood neighborhood, and the old Chicago Mercantile Exchange (1927) at 110 North Franklin Street. Here, on the historic site of Fort Dearborn, he designed a 22-story Indiana limestone building using classical references throughout, from the three-story columns marking the entrance, repeated above the fifteenth floor, to the Greco-Roman tempietto on top. This aesthetic is consistent with Burnham's 1909 Plan of Chicago, which envisioned the development of the riverfront in the grand Beaux Arts tradition. Note how the rusticated base matches that of the Wacker Drive Esplanade below and how the unusual concave facade accommodates the semicircular plaza defining the intersection of Michigan Avenue with Wacker Drive.

Holabird and Root
1927–8

The last-built of the four original buildings located at the Michigan Avenue Bridge, 333 North Michigan Avenue resembles a slender gatepost when seen from the length of North Michigan Avenue. Clad in granite and limestone, its design reflects the sleek, Art Deco aesthetic of its time: the mass of the eleven-story tower rising from the 24-story main block is modified by a series of setbacks that emphasize its verticality, as does the absence of a cornice. At the fifth floor of the building are a series of seven-foot-high bas-reliefs by sculptor Fred M. Torrey, depicting the growth and early history of Chicago: The Portage, the Hunter, Pioneer Women, the Attack on Fort Dearborn, the Covered Wagon Era, and the Traders. These reliefs harmonize with the overall massing of the building in their bold, simplified lines; they also typify the interest of the era in incorporating sculptural design into the architectural program. Holabird and Root, formed in 1928, was the successor firm to Holabird and Roche and continues to practice today. Its notable designs include the Palmolive Building (see #41), the Chicago Daily News Building (1925–9) (see Riverfront, #20), and the Chicago Board of Trade (1929–30) (see Loop, #8).

Edward H. Bennett, architect; Thomas Pihlfeldt, engineer of bridges; Hugh Young, engineer of bridge design; Henry Herring and J. E. Fraser, sculptors
Michigan Avenue and the Chicago River
1918–20; pylon sculptures, 1928

The Michigan Avenue Bridge blended the Beaux Arts aesthetics of Daniel Burnham's 1909 Plan of Chicago with the sophisticated engineering necessary to solve one of Chicago's worst transportation problems. Before 1920, when Michigan Avenue still ended at the river, nearly half of Chicago's north-south traffic converged at the old Rush Street swing bridge, which was also among the first bridges encountered by ships entering from the lake. To ease the resulting congestion, Chicago engineers perfected a bridge type in which leaves divide, rotate around a trunnion pin, and return to their fixed positions. The Michigan Avenue Bridge was their masterpiece: the world's first double-leaf, double-deck trunnion bascule bridge, capable of handling two levels of traffic and still clearing the channel in under 60 seconds. Much of Burnham's grand, classical design, modeled after the Seine bridges of Paris, was implemented after Burnham's death by Edward Bennett (1874–1954), consultant to the Chicago Plan Commission. Bennett's four limestone bridge houses create a monumental approach to this important crossing, while commemorative sculptures by J. E. Fraser and Henry Herring mark the historic location, spanning the sites of Fort Dearborn and Chicago's first pioneer homesteads.

Graham, Anderson, Probst and White
410 North Michigan Avenue
1919–22 (south tower); 1924–5 (north tower)

The Wrigley Building may be Chicago's favorite landmark. Its gleaming white facade and gently curving entrance plaza convey a bright, welcoming feeling; most familiar of all is the eleven-story clocktower, inspired by the Giralda Tower in Seville, Spain, which has also been spotlit at night from the outset. The building was developed by William Wrigley, founder of the chewing gum company, and remains the Wrigley Company headquarters today. As the first building completed north of the Chicago River on the newly extended Michigan Avenue, it initiated the area's redevelopment from a dingy warehouse district to a desirable commercial address. A second building was added to the north in 1925, and is connected to the first at the lobby and by an upper-level skywalk. Both are sheathed in terra cotta, a material popular both for its decorative potential, and for its fire-proofing ability, not underestimated in a city leveled by fire just 50 years before. To encourage public access to the Chicago River, a monumental staircase was designed that leads from the entrance plaza to a riverside landing where tour boats dock in the summertime.

Skidmore, Owings & Merrill
401 North Michigan Avenue
1962–5

On this site, pioneer Jean Baptiste du Sable, Chicago's first permanent settler, built his cabin. Now a 35-story office tower of glazed bronze solar glass with an aluminum curtain wall rises, recalling the structurally expressive style of noted architect Ludwig Mies van der Rohe (1886–1969). This aesthetic was often used by Skidmore, Owings & Merrill in its commercial high-rise designs. Here design partner Bruce Graham (b. 1925) used granite spandrels to mark the floors, while slender vertical piers containing circular pipes divide the windows into sets of four. This pattern gives the facade a subtle rhythm, enhanced when the Chicago River is reflected in the glass. The Chicago Tribune sold the land to the Equitable Life Assurance Society on condition that the new structure be no taller than the Tribune Tower and that, set back from Michigan Avenue, it not obstruct the Tribune's views. Pioneer Court, a plaza connecting the two buildings, is often used for summertime art exhibitions; via a sweeping spiral staircase, it also provides public access to the riverbank below. Such access was an amenity envisioned in the 1909 Plan of Chicago by architects Daniel Burnham and Edward Bennett.

Tower, Hood and Howells; printing plant, Jarvis Hunt
435 North Michigan Avenue
Tower, 1922–5; printing plant, 1916–20

In 1922, the Chicago Tribune announced what became one of the twentieth century's most famous architectural competitions: $100,000 in prize money to design its new headquarters on a site near the just-completed Michigan Avenue Bridge and adjacent to the Tribune's new printing plant on the Chicago River, where the waterway facilitated shipment of newsprint and other operations. The 264 competition entries from around the world, included a fascinating range of designs for "the world's most beautiful office building." The winning entry, by Raymond Hood and John Mead Howells of New York, dresses a plain limestone shaft with the gargoyle gutters and flamboyant flying buttresses of France's great Gothic cathedrals. The grand arched entry and surrounding allegorical figures are impressive, but the tower steals the scene: a crown of open tracery that remains as visible and photogenic today as it was in 1922. Ironically, the contest's most influential entry may not have been the winner, but Finnish architect Eliel Saarinen's second-place design. Its strongly rooted and elegantly set-back mass helped define the skyscraper form for the rest of the century. Hood himself referred to it in his later designs in New York for the Daily News Building and Rockefeller Center complex.

Walter W. Alschlager
505 North Michigan Avenue
1929
Now known as the Inter-Continental Hotel

Originally the private, men-only Medinah Athletic Club, this 45-story limestone building was commissioned at the height of the 1920s by the Medinah Nobles, an affiliate of the Shriners with purported roots in the Middle East. Its exotic, eclectic design reflects these presumed origins: note the gold onion dome at the top, and the Assyrian and Egyptian figures carved by Leon Harmart (1866–1936) that grace the facade. These relief sculptures celebrate the builder's trade and the legendary origin of the Freemasons (or stonemasons) guild in England, a forerunner of the Shriners' philanthropic organization, which is known today for its circus and hospitals. Inside, public rooms range in style from an English Tudor Hall to a Spanish Tea Court to a five-story Stair Hall of Lions. Athletic facilities, unmatched at the time of completion, included a rifle range and miniature golf courses. A thorough renovation, sensitive to the building's stylistic eccentricity, was recently completed by Harry Weese and Associates. Today, the Hotel Inter-Continental is an exuberant, idiosyncratic complement to neighboring 1920s designs, the famous Tribune Tower (see #26) next door and the Wrigley Building (see #24) across the avenue.

Thielbar and Fugard
520 North Michigan Avenue
1927–9

Designed by Chicago architects Frederick J. Thielbar and John Reed Fugard, the McGraw-Hill Building is a collaboration between one of the city's leading architectural firms and the sculptors Eugene and Gwen Lux. Gwen Lux (1908–86) is among America's pioneer women sculptors; her work can be found at the Rockefeller Center complex in New York City and at the General Motors Technical Center, designed by architect Eero Saarinen, in Detroit. Note the series of limestone panels depicting figures of Greek mythology and the zodiac. The McGraw-Hill Building served as the midwestern headquarters for the McGraw-Hill publishing company. This elegant limestone Art Deco tower also exemplifies the development of Michigan Avenue north of the Chicago River in the 1920s after the opening of the Michigan Avenue Bridge. Michigan Avenue became the location of choice for midwestern offices of New York City corporations. The North Central Association, now the Greater North Michigan Avenue Association, worked closely with architects and developers to ensure the highest-quality design and uses for the new, European-inspired boulevard.

Marshall and Fox
601 North Michigan Avenue
1921–2
Now known as The First National Bank

Benjamin Marshall (1874–1924) and Charles Fox (1870–1926) founded their firm in 1905 and enjoyed great success in Chicago, especially after World War I. Their clientele included well-heeled families and establishments: they designed the Drake Hotel (see #43) on North Michigan Avenue and the lakefront, and today Marshall's luxury apartment buildings on nearby East Lake Shore Drive form the nucleus of the East Lake Shore Drive Historic District. The Lake Shore Trust and Savings Bank has a five-story limestone facade with full-height Corinthian columns flanked by rectangular piers that anchor the building. Many banks are classically styled, but here the cubic envelope creates a simple volume that is stripped of extraneous elements, such as pediments, sculptural reliefs, or figures. The Lake Shore Trust and Savings Bank was organized by prominent members of the North Central Business District Association, many of whom were real estate developers. In this bank, they found a forthright expression to symbolize their financial faith in the new North Michigan Avenue and in Chicago's future.

Philip Brooks Maher
626 North Michigan Avenue
1926

Familiar with a range of historical styles and skilled at using them effectively, architect Philip Brooks Maher adapted French Second Empire forms for this building, contributing to the Parisian-influenced development of North Michigan Avenue in the 1920s. Maher (1894–1981), the son of Prairie School architect George W. Maher, designed more buildings on North Michigan Avenue than anyone but the large firm Holabird and Root. Many of these structures have been demolished, but the Farwell building (see #32) and this building remain. In this nine-story structure, home to the country's oldest women's athletic facility, a number of nonathletic functions were accommodated. The first floor was devoted to swank retail shops; the second, or *piano nobile*, was reserved for public occasions; the crowning seventh and eighth floors were designed for a grand ballroom in which large social gatherings were held. The window treatments mark these special uses: a Palladian window heralds the second floor on Ontario Street, while on the upper stories niches housing winged griffins flank large windows decorated with swags and bucrania (ox skulls with garland-festooned horns). Other ornamental details include bands of anthemion and acanthus leaves, favorite classical motifs.

Solomon Cordwell Buenz & Associates
646 North Michigan Avenue
1990

Crate & Barrel's flagship store is distinguished by its low-scale, sleek alternating horizontal bands of glass and shiny white aluminum, and a full-height, glass-enclosed corner rotunda. Escalators were placed in the transparent rotunda to maximize merchandising space on the small site and to draw customers to its upper floors; during the crowded holiday season, passengers seem to glide from floor to floor like colorful ribbons. The curved corner element becomes the fulcrum of the plan, radiating along both Michigan Avenue and Erie Street, reminiscent of Louis Sullivan's Carson Pirie Scott store at the corner of State and Madison Streets in the Loop. Although the exterior contrasts in color and material with the masonry Woman's Athletic Club next door (see #30), both buildings are similar in height, so a street wall continuity is maintained. Such low-scale development is especially welcome, given the huge towers that have been developed on Michigan Avenue since the late 1960s. The interior, designed in cooperation with Ray Arenson of Crate & Barrel, is sheathed in light knotty pine to convey a neutral background for the clean, modern home products displayed here.

664–70 North Michigan Avenue
664 North Michigan Avenue, 1927: Philip B. Maher
Renovation of 664 and 666 North Michigan Avenue:
Booth Hansen & Associates, 1987

The Terra Museum of American Art, designed to house Daniel Terra's collection of American art, is planned as a three-phase project, corresponding to the three adjacent buildings being renovated for this purpose. The southernmost among them is the Farwell Building, an eleven-story Bedford limestone structure designed in an attenuated Beaux Arts style. The building retains its ground-floor retail space, but Terra's collection occupies the four floors above; the remaining floors are used for museum offices and storage. The central and principal structure was formerly the Helene Curtis cosmetics salon; this five-story building now faced in gray-veined white Vermont marble. It houses the museum's main entrance hall, a bookshop, and a central atrium. These two buildings connect by means of interior curved ramps, required for handicap access, but also creating a decorative pattern as seen from Michigan Avenue through 45-foot-high glass walls. The northernmost of the three buildings is a four-story medical arts building, earmarked for a planned expansion of museum facilities. Culture, commerce, and tourism create a powerful synergy on this prestigious boulevard. It is no wonder that Michigan Avenue was the choice for one of Chicago's newest museums.

Murgatroyd and Ogden
Associate Architects, Fugard and Knapp
701 North Michigan Avenue
1924
Now known as the Allerton Hotel

Built in the North Italian Renaissance style, with a central tower flanked by four smaller towers and a series of arched windows and corbeled sills, this 25-story building was among the first to be completed on North Michigan Avenue and was under construction at the same time as the nearby Tribune Tower (see #26). Although the shaft of the hotel is red brick, its three-story limestone base harmonizes with other limestone buildings that were being built or planned for the new avenue. Ground-floor retail space is on the Michigan Avenue side while the two-story, triple-arched entrance is on Huron Street. Inside, a grand two-story limestone stairwell continues the stylistic theme. Modeled on the Barbizon Hotel and other Allerton "Clubs" that catered to young professional men and women, the building combined the amenities of a private club and a hotel. For instance, it originally had a rooftop eighteen-hole golf course and handball court, workout rooms on every floor, a library, weekly dancing and card parties, and even an Allerton Glee Club. Fourteen floors were designated for men and six floors for women, who used a separate elevator bank.

Skidmore, Owings & Merrill
737 North Michigan Avenue
1978–86

This mixed-use building of pink Swedish granite is among several designed by Skidmore, Owings & Merrill on North Michigan Avenue (see #40 and #44). It combines the low-rise, four-story Neiman Marcus Department Store facing Michigan Avenue and a 63-story tower with office and residential use configured on a north/south axis and entered on Chicago Avenue. The height of the Michigan Avenue section respects the context and memory of a lower-scale street, where wide sidewalks and ground-floor retail encourage pedestrian use. Notable is the grand two-story entrance arch; though non–load bearing, it recalls the language of such Chicago School buildings as the Rookery and the Auditorium Building (see #3). Its "keystone" is a glass slit connecting to an arched skylight. Note the coffered underside of the arch, with its backlit, translucent glass. The tapering of the tower results from the greater size requirements for office space, while the 200 condominiums above have smaller floorplates but larger windows. Architect Adrian Smith (b. 1944) is known for his evocative interpretations of the past, which are blended with state-of-the-art structural systems, here developed by engineer and SOM partner, Fazlur Khan.

Robert A. M. Stern Architects
744 North Michigan Avenue
1991

What would Daniel Burnham think? Rather than the Beaux Arts buildings envisioned in the 1909 Plan of Chicago for North Michigan Avenue, this imaginative renovation of an existing concrete frame structure instead recalls prefabricated metal structures once exported from Europe to tropical colonies abroad. The entire two-story facade is covered in panels of lead-coated copper; an eyebrow window peeks above its barrel-vaulted roof. Wide sidewalks on North Michigan Avenue allow a miniature landscaped setting of twin green squares to frame the entrance. As a build-to-suit for clothier Banana Republic, which sells moderately-priced casual safari-style wear, the interior design is critical to the building's success. The most dramatic feature greeting customers is a double-return staircase with latticed leather balusters suspended by a series of guyed cables underneath a gabled skylight. Furniture and accessories follow the elegant, exotic theme: sisal rugs, wood, leather tile flooring, suede armchairs, metal lighting fixtures, and earthenware urns. New York architect Robert A. M. Stern (b. 1939) is among America's best-known practitioners, with a wide range of designs from luxurious residences to resort hotels for the Walt Disney Company. This is his only Chicago building.

W. W. Boyington
800 North Michigan Avenue; 163 East Pearson Street
1867–9

The Water Tower was the pride of Chicago when completed in 1869, housing the technology required to provide an adequate water supply to the growing young city in a dignified "castellated Gothic" structure. The tower contained the 138-foot standpipe needed to equalize the pressure of the eighteen million gallons of water pumped daily from the squat pumping station on the east side of Michigan Avenue. Naively Gothic in form, the tower rises from a foursquare plan with identical facades, corner turrets, crenellated battlements, and slit windows. Note the crude window architraves and the contrast of the tower's green copper cap with the sunny rusticated limestone from Joliet, Illinois. When the water tower survived the Chicago Fire of 1871, it became a symbol of the city's rebuilding spirit and energy. Indeed, the planners who widened Pine Street in 1918 to create the new North Michigan Avenue angled the street's path to sidestep these structures. The tower became functionally obsolete long ago, but has been preserved and serves today as a visitor information center. The pumping station still pumps water for the central city. Nestled amidst North Michigan Avenue's sophisticated hustle, they remain important connections to the city's past.

Josef Paul Kleihues
234 East Chicago Ave.
1996

The five-story, 151,000-square-foot Museum of Contemporary Art by German architect Josef Paul Kleihues (b. 1933) is five times the size of the museum's former home. Its one-acre sculpture garden takes advantage of the spectacular site overlooking Lake Michigan just east of the historic Chicago Water Tower and Pumping Station (see #36) that survived the 1871 Chicago Fire. One of the most striking features of Chicago's newest museum is its soaring 56-foot-high glass-fronted facade, which is set above a sixteen-foot base of Indiana limestone and provides views of two levels of the interior. Also unusual are the hand-cast aluminum panels fastened with stainless steel buttons to the facade. The ground floor houses support space, a 15,000-square-foot education center, and the museum store. Two-story-high gallery spaces on the second floor house temporary exhibitions. Another level of galleries, located on the fourth floor, includes barrel-vaulted skylights and is devoted primarily to the museum's permanent collection. A restaurant and special events space run the width of the building's eastern facade, with views of the sculpture garden and Lake Michigan beyond.

Loebl Schlossman Dart and Hackl,
with C. F. Murphy Associates
845 North Michigan Avenue
1976

This mixed-use structure combines a seven-story vertical shopping mall, office space, the Ritz-Carlton Hotel lobby area, and a 62-story, 859-foot tower that contains hotel rooms and 200 condominiums. The shopping mall has a large atrium with glass elevators rising dramatically through it. Over 100 shops as well as restaurants and theaters are contained within its 610,000 square feet. To maximize rentable space, the mall has blank walls above the ground-floor windows, turning its back on one of Chicago's great streets. At street level, however, its escalators are visible though the ground-floor windows, funneling consumers to its treasures within. The mixed-use program, seen also in Olympia Centre (see #34), One Magnificent Mile (see #44), and 900 North Michigan Avenue (see #42), is still searching for its form. Here, a low-scale box is attached to a tower behind it. Once considered a daring venture, since it brought a suburban mall concept to the heart of the city, the interior shopping area has precedents in Chicago in several nineteenth-century skyscrapers that were organized around interior atria as well as the more recent, but now destroyed, Diana Court in Holabird and Root's Michigan Square Building (1928).

Ralph Adams Cram
125 East Chestnut Street
1912–4
Manse, Parish House, Cloister, and Blair Chapel
Howard Van Doren Shaw
1925

The first Presbyterian congregation in Chicago was organized in 1833, the same year Chicago became a town. The Fourth Presbyterian Church represents a consolidation of various congregations and was built on land made available by the McCormicks, wealthy church parishioners. When it opened in 1914, North Michigan Avenue, then called Pine Street, was little more than a dirt road along the marshy shoreline, and the church overlooked Lake Michigan instead of the John Hancock Center (see #40). Ralph Adams Cram (1862–1945), architect of the Cathedral of St. John the Divine in New York City, designed this church in the English Perpendicular Gothic style, with its requisite carved ornament: crockets on the arches, spire, and pinnacle, quatrefoils and cinquefoils in the window tracery. The building is uniform in plan and constructed of gray Bedford limestone; its verticality is emphasized by its 122-foot spire and by the narrow lancet windows of its belfry. The facade of the sanctuary is composed of two monumental compound pointed arches, the lower housing the double entrance doors, the upper framing a large stained glass window. Adjacent to the church and connected to it by an ivy-covered cloister are the parish house and manse, designed by Howard Van Doren Shaw, complementing the church.

Skidmore, Owings & Merrill
870 North Michigan Avenue
1964–70

Like a giant bridge set on its side, the 100-story John Hancock Center is marked by huge X-braces that stiffen the structure against wind forces while forming a distinctive pattern on its surface. Controversial from the start for its enormous hulk and dark metal cladding, this mixed-use project, combining retail, residential, and office space, broke all the rules of its genteel, mostly low-rise Michigan Avenue neighborhood. It was soon celebrated for its very brashness, however, becoming a Chicago icon complete with a nickname: "Big John." Engineer Fazlur Khan (1929–82), working with architect Bruce Graham, devised the ingenious "braced tube" system, carrying loads downward so efficiently that only 29.7 pounds of steel per square foot were required, a third less than in comparable buildings. These exterior tubes support the structure, necessitating no interior columns. The building occupies only 50 percent of its full-block site; a plaza on Michigan Avenue occupies the other half, providing an open space for pedestrians and a showcase for the skyscraper. A recent renovation has revitalized the street and concourse levels by clarifying entrances and creating inviting spaces for relaxing and dining.

Holabird and Root
919 North Michigan Avenue
1927–9
Now known by its address

Six symmetrical setbacks sculpt the mass of this 37-story Indiana limestone high-rise that once dominated the vista on Michigan Avenue north of the Chicago River. The site, a mile north of the Loop business district, was selected by the Palm-Olive-Peet Company because of its dramatic lakefront views and prestigious surroundings adjacent to the residential Gold Coast. Vertical piers alternate with recessed, window-filled channels, creating a regular rhythm on the facade that carries the eye upward. Exterior decoration is limited to incised designs on piers and entrances. Lighting is another key element of the Art Deco style; here, electrical floodlights emphasize the powerful setbacks. For over 50 years it had a powerful beacon on its rooftop to guide aerial and maritime traffic; eventually it became a nuisance as other towers arose nearby. Combining grace and power with masterful planning on an exceptional site, this structure is considered among the best of Holabird and Root's work. John Augur Holabird (1886–1945) and John Wellborn Root, Jr. (1887–1963) were sons of prominent Chicago architects William Holabird (1854–1923) and John Wellborn Root (1850–91). They joined the firm Holabird and Roche in 1919, renaming it Holabird and Root upon the death of the senior partners.

Kohn Pedersen Fox
Associate Architects, Perkins & Will
1983–9

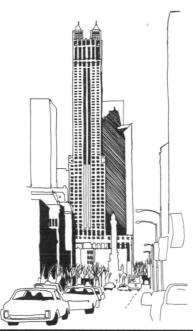

Among the most recent and largest mixed-use projects on Michigan Avenue, this building adheres to the box-plus-tower concept to address its complex programmatic requirements of retail, office, hotel, condominium, and parking facilities. Like its sister center Water Tower Place (see #38), developed a decade earlier, the vertical retail mall is contained in an eight-story cube that preserves the low-scale character of Michigan Avenue at street level. Above, its setback tower is a sentinel for the view north on the Avenue, much as 333 North Michigan Avenue is to the south, creating both a personality and an identity for their portions of the famous street. The structural engineering of this building combines two systems: steel for the lower twenty stories of retail and office sections and a concrete tube above, which allows more open floor plates. The retail base contains the interior shopping mall, including Bloomingdale's, for which the retail complex is named. Above the base are the Four Seasons Hotel, guest room floors, office floors, and residential apartments. The entrance is marked by a huge round portal through which are views of the shopping atrium, and the top is crowned with four corner pavilions and lanterns.

Marshall and Fox
140 East Walton Street
1919

Overlooking Oak Street Beach, where the residential Gold Coast meets fashionable North Michigan Avenue, the 800-room Drake Hotel represents subdued elegance and comfort. Inspired by Italian Renaissance palazzos, architects Benjamin Marshall and Charles Fox punctuated the sheer limestone walls with regularly spaced windows and Renaissance decorative motifs such as consoles and garlands. The main reception rooms are located, Italian-style, on a *piano nobile*, and windows here are capped by alternating round and flattened arches. Above the Lake Shore Drive entrance, a colonnade connects the two side wings; inside is a two-story grand ballroom with oversized columns. The Drake, designed in an H-shaped block to maximize exterior views, offered large family apartment units, an entire floor for bachelors, and first-class accommodations. Completed just before the opening of the Michigan Avenue Bridge in 1920, it was among the first buildings constructed on the new thoroughfare that replaced narrow Pine Street, which was broadened and renamed North Michigan Avenue. Its developers, John B. and Tracy C. Drake earlier developed the Blackstone Hotel (see #2), also designed by Marshall and Fox, as was the Lake Shore Trust and Savings Bank (see #29).

Skidmore, Owings & Merrill
940–80 North Michigan Avenue
1978–83

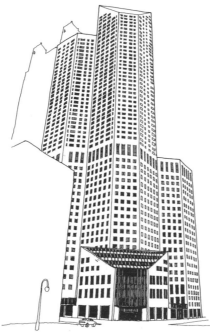

One Magnificent Mile is a showcase of the possibilities of the bundled-tube structural system, pioneered by the talented team of engineer Fazlur Khan and architect Bruce Graham. Khan was a partner at Skidmore, Owings & Merrill, and one of the country's most innovative structural engineers. He collaborated with Graham on the John Hancock Center (see #40) and the Sears Tower (1974), and with Adrian Smith on Olympia Centre (see #34). Here, three hexagonal concrete tubes with punched window openings rise 57, 49, and 21 stories, respectively, and are joined as a bundled tube to resist wind loads. The perimeter tubes eliminated structural cores, allowing uninterrupted floorspans. Residential condominiums are above the two-story mechanical floors at the 21-story line; offices are below, with retail on the first three levels. Its distinctive shape was chosen in order to meet several criteria: maximizing size while minimizing shadows that would fall on nearby Oak Street Park Beach; relating to other neighboring buildings, as befits a corner site; and creating a distinctive gateway to the city's prestigious retail corridor. For example, note how its six-story sloped entrance nods toward the Drake Hotel across Michigan Avenue (see #43) instead of overwhelming it with taller elements at the street edge.

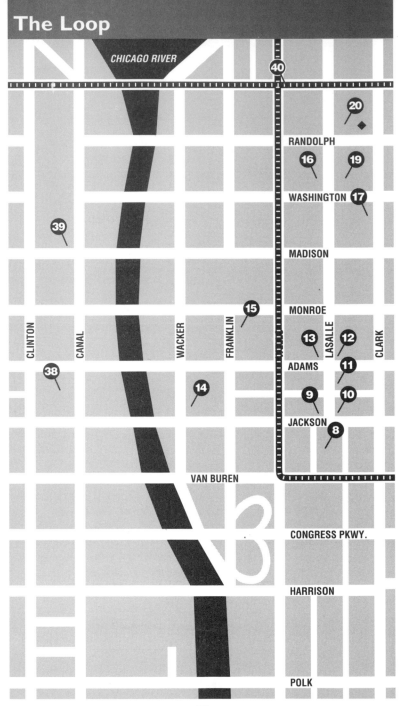

The Loop

CHICAGO RIVER

RANDOLPH

WASHINGTON

MADISON

MONROE

ADAMS

JACKSON

VAN BUREN

CONGRESS PKWY.

HARRISON

POLK

CLINTON

CANAL

WACKER

FRANKLIN

LASALLE

CLARK

WABASH

LAKE

CLARK

DEARBORN

STATE

EAST BALBO

1 Harold Washington Library Center
2 Leiter Building
3 Manhattan Building
4 Old Colony Building
5 William J. Campbell U.S. Courthouse Annex
6 Monadnock Building
7 Fisher Building
8 Chicago Board of Trade
9 Federal Reserve Bank
10 Continental Illinois National Bank
11 Rookery
12 Field Building
13 190 South LaSalle Street
14 Sears Tower
15 AT&T Corporate Center
16 120 North LaSalle Street
17 Conway Building
18 The Chicago Temple Building
◆ Miro's Chicago, 1981, Joan Miro
19 City and County Building
20 State of Illinois Center
◆ Monument with Standing Beast, 1984, Jean Dubuffet
21 Richard J. Daley Center
◆ Chicago Picasso, 1967, Pablo Picasso
22 Chicago Theatre
23 Page Brothers Building
24 SelfPark
25 Marshall Field and Company Store
26 Reliance Building
27 Carson Pirie Scott and Company
28 Chicago Building
29 Inland Steel
30 First National Bank Building
◆ The Four Seasons, 1974, Marc Chagall
31 Xerox Centre
32 The Marquette Building
33 Federal Center
◆ Flamingo, 1974, Alexander Calder
34 The Berghoff
35 Pontiac Building
36 Franklin Building
37 Dearborn Street Station
38 Union Station
39 Northwestern Atrium
40 The Loop Elevated

Hammond, Beeby and Babka

Full block bounded by State Street, Congress Parkway, Plymouth Court, and Van Buren Street

1989–91

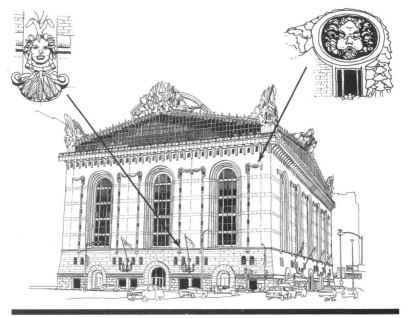

Named in honor of Chicago's first black mayor, Harold Washington, this ten-story, 756,640-square-foot red granite and brick building is the largest public library in the United States. Its Postmodern design won a highly publicized architectural competition in 1988 and recalls significant Chicago School of Architecture buildings: the three-story rusticated stone base reflects the Rookery (see #11), the deeply recessed arched windows are inspired by the nearby Auditorium Building, and the sloping brick midsection recalls the Monadnock Building (see #6). As in the City and County Building (see #19), the building's civic nature is identified by the monumental scale of its elements. Further, Chicago iconography enlivens the facade: Ceres, goddess of grain, wears a necklace of corn tied with a ribbon inscribed with the city's motto, "Urbs in Horto," while above, festoons are anchored by medallions with the Chicago River "Y" and a "Windy City" head. Administrative offices and a wintergarden occupy the top floor, where intersecting metal and glass barrel vaults offer natural light and structural drama. Service facilities are located on the perimeter of the glass-sided west wall facing Plymouth Court. The building interior is arranged on a generous 21-foot column grid, providing flexibility for the library's changing needs.

William Le Baron Jenney
403 South State Street
1891
Now known as the Second Leiter Building

Occupying a full block at Congress Parkway and State Street, the eight-story, 553,000-square-foot Second Leiter Building was advertised as the largest retail establishment in the world when completed. It was excellent investment for Levi Z. Leiter, who in 1881 left his partnership with merchandiser Marshall Field to become a real estate developer. The building was first leased to Siegel, Cooper and Company; Sears, Roebuck and Company occupied it 1932–1978. Though William Le Baron Jenney (1832–1907) developed a successful architectural practice in Chicago, he was trained as a civil engineer and served with the Union Army Corps of Engineers during the Civil War. Some historians consider this building Jenney's most successful work because the clarity of its design matches his engineering skill. The well-proportioned gray Maine granite facade is a straightforward expression of the underlying steel grid. Smooth, slender piers stretch the eye upward and give the building lightness; wide horizontal glass expanses let the large mass breathe. Minimal interior columns and sixteen-foot ceilings created open floors where merchandise could be effectively displayed. Thus the building met the needs of the architectural program while creating an aesthetically pleasing composition.

William Le Baron Jenney
431 South Dearborn Street
1889–91; Renovation: Hasbrouck-Hunderman
1982

William Le Baron Jenney's office was a center for young architects who came to Chicago to rebuild the city after the 1871 fire: Louis Sullivan, William Holabird, Daniel Burnham, and Martin Roche all apprenticed there. Jenney is best known for his Home Insurance Company Building (1885, destroyed), which first used the steel skeleton frame to support an exterior wall. His Manhattan Building illustrates the integration of several additional technological innovations that made further development of the modern skyscraper possible. First, since the structure was sandwiched between two smaller buildings, he had to lessen the loads on the party walls. To do so, he set the Manhattan Building back at the tenth floor, thus designing the first setback skyscraper. Second, he adapted knee and portal bracing from bridge construction to gird the building against the wind. Third, he developed a system of hangers to attach the masonry units to the frame of each floor, allowing them to shift with the movement of the skeleton frame. Thus, although the confused facade reflects uncertainty about the appropriate exterior expression for this new building type, many elements of today's skyscrapers are already addressed in this early commercial high-rise.

Holabird and Roche
407 South Dearborn Street
1893–4

The Old Colony stands among a distinguished group of early skyscrapers along South Dearborn Street: the Manhattan Building, the Monadnock Building, and the Fisher Building. There are no masonry bearing walls in this building, and the internal structure of the building is visible in the window grid pattern on the broad limestone facades along Dearborn Street and Plymouth Court. On the building's shorter sides, Chicago windows are flanked by double-hung windows in a rhythm punctuated by the rounded bay windows that wrap around the corners to admit additional light and air to the building. The Old Colony's seventeen-story height required a wind-bracing system that includes four sets of portal arches that extend from the foundation to the roof and brace the horizontal and vertical structural elements. Built on speculation by Boston lawyer Francis Bartlett, the building was named for the first English colony in America at Plymouth, Massachusetts. Note its seal carved in stone at the entrance. The building was a successful venture, offering 600 offices that were occupied by railroad, printing, and lumber interests who sought space here in the thriving printing center of the Midwest.

5 William J. Campbell U. S. Courthouse Annex

Harry Weese and Associates
71 West Van Buren Street
1973–5

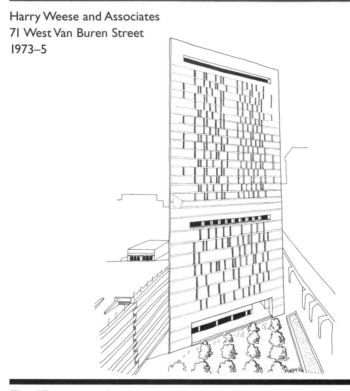

This 27-story reinforced concrete tower, also known as the Metropolitan Correctional Center, was planned for those awaiting trial on federal charges and is unique in several respects. Detention centers are rarely placed in business district locations or housed in skyscrapers. Yet Harry Weese's (b. 1915) inventive design accommodates both the rigorous program requirements necessary to house inmates and the context of the historic south Loop location. The triangular configuration minimizes corridor lengths for guards while providing maximum perimeter space for windows, each of which is five inches wide, the largest allowed by Bureau of Prison standards. These openings form an interesting, computer-punch-card-like abstract pattern on the smooth facade. Lower floors function as administrative and social service areas, while the upper levels are for inmates. Each multipurpose core space serves 44 people and is divided into a two-story unit, with inmates' rooms arranged around common lounge, dining, and visitors' facilities. In good weather, note the inmates using the roof-top exercise yard. At the building's base, the landscaped plaza creates an inviting entrance typical of many office buildings in the area. Original and efficient, this building is among Weese's most thoughtful designs.

Northern half: Burnham and Root
Southern half: Holabird and Roche
53 West Jackson Boulevard
Northern half, 1891;
southern half, 1893

Initially planned as four connected buildings, the Monadnock Building, in its unadorned functionalism, embodies Chicago commercial architecture. It was developed on a narrow 400- by 68-foot lot by Bostonians Peter and Shepherd Brooks, with Owen Aldis as their Chicago agent, and is named after Mount Monadnock in New Hampshire. In the northern section, John Root (1850–91) of Burnham & Root, who had also designed the Rookery for the Brooks brothers, maximized rentable space by stretching the building to an unheard-of sixteen stories and punching out a grid of bay windows that also added light and ventilation. To support this height, exterior masonry walls six feet thick at the base were required. Note how the curve of the corners is repeated in the cavetto cornice. After Root's death in 1891, the firm of Holabird and Roche was hired to develop the southern half of the block. Here, in the last quadrant, the building is supported by the new steel frame construction, rather than the old-fashioned masonry bearing wall. Thus, in this massive block, constructed over a period of three years, we can see the end of one era in construction and the beginning of another.

D. H. Burnham and Co.
343 South Dearborn Street
1895–6; addition, 1906

The eighteen-story Fisher Building was among the tallest commercial structures in the world when it was completed in 1896. Charles Atwood (1840–95) is credited with the design; Edward Shankland (1854–1924), with the construction. The building combines inventive structural solutions with fanciful ornament. Steel columns were riveted together to form continuous rigid supports, an efficient construction method that allowed the entire frame to be erected in a month. The foundation required to support such a tall building on Chicago's swampy soil presented another challenge. The solution was to drive groups of massive piles 40 feet underground surmounted by a pyramid of I-beams laid in cross section and filled with Portland cement. The exterior reveals a distinctive interplay between glass and rich golden terra-cotta ornament. Note the playful marine shapes on the lower floors that refer to the building's owner, Lucius G. Fisher, while above, whimsical creatures creep and slither along Gothic arches and window sills, evidence of Atwood's exuberant imagination. Terra cotta was also used inside the building, where it sheaths the flat steel arches supporting the floors. The three-bay addition to the north was designed by Peter J. Weber (1864–1923), also of Burnham's office.

Holabird and Root
141 West Jackson Boulevard
1929–30
Addition: Murphy/Jahn with
Shaw and Associates and
Swanke, Hayden, Connell Architects
1980

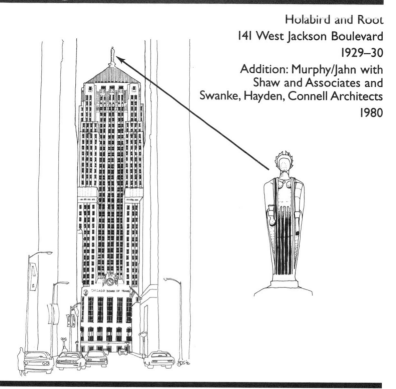

The Chicago Board of Trade stands in the center of LaSalle Street, at once proclaiming the centrality of nature's bounty to Chicago's economy and the human ability to abstract nature into a sophisticated trading mechanism. The first Board of Trade on this site was designed by W. W. Boyington (1818–98) in 1885. The present structure is a 45-story limestone Art Deco skyscraper, for a quarter century the tallest building in Chicago. Thirty-story wings flank the nine-story base, above which rises a central clock adorned with Alvin Meyer's sculpted allegorical figures: a hooded figure for wheat and an Indian with corn, representing the grains of the Old World and the New. John Storr's aluminum Ceres, goddess of agriculture, tops the metal pyramidal roof. The spacious two-story interior of the lobby is detailed with scalloped curves, metal banding, and dramatic lighting. Fifty years after the building's completion another trading floor was needed, as well as new offices for the Chicago commodities exchange. Architect Helmut Jahn's (b. 1940) 24-story addition reinterprets the original building's massing in glass and steel. Note John Warner Norton's mural of Ceres that once graced the original trading floor and now hangs in the addition's spectacular twelve-story atrium.

Graham, Anderson, Probst and White
230 South LaSalle Street
1920–2
Southwestern addition: Naess and Murphy, 1957;
northwestern addition: Holabird and Root, 1984–9

Dignified and imposing, the sixteen-story limestone Federal Reserve Bank houses the Chicago branch of the central banking system. Together with its "twin" across the street (see #10), it forms a symmetrical end to LaSalle Street at the Chicago Board of Trade (see #8). Six massive Corinthian columns topped by a pediment mark the LaSalle Street entrance. Above them the exterior is plain, but the interior is not. Its grand three-story banking hall was renovated by Holabird and Root in the 1980s and opened to the street level to provide a spectacular four-level entrance lobby. The renovation also included a fourteen-story addition on the northwest corner of the site, a new limestone cladding on the 1957 addition, and a complete reorganization of the building's internal work and traffic flow. In addition to office space, the building also includes banking and check processing operations, warehousing, and safekeeping areas. This structure was one of seven Federal Reserve Bank buildings designed by Graham, Anderson, Probst and White during the 1920s, evidence of the firm's ability to provide expressive form for America's financial establishment.

Graham, Anderson, Probst and White
231 South LaSalle Street
1923–4
Formerly the Illinois Merchants Bank

The Federal Reserve Bank (see #9) and the Continental Illinois National Bank directly across LaSalle Street were designed by the same firm and share many similarities: massing, proportions, materials, and the style so often associated with financial institutions, the dignified Greek temple. Here, the entrance is marked by six Ionic columns supporting the pediment, while, on the interior, 28 Ionic columns line the magnificent two-story banking room that stretches across the entire length of the building on the second floor. Note the murals painted by Jules Guerin (1866–1946), perhaps best known for his renderings that accompanied Daniel H. Burnham's 1909 Plan of Chicago. Graham, Anderson, Probst and White, was the second successor firm to D. H. Burnham and Company. When Daniel Burnham died in 1912, Ernest Graham (1868–1936) assumed leadership of the prolific firm known for its Beaux Arts aesthetic and large-scale projects. Peirce Anderson (1870–1924), Edward Probst (1870–1942), and Howard Judson White (1870–1936) joined him as partners five years later. In Chicago, their work includes such landmarks as The Wrigley Building, the Merchandise Mart, the Field Museum of Natural History, and Union Station (see #38).

Burnham and Root
209 South LaSalle Street
1885–8
Lobby renovation: Frank Lloyd Wright, 1905; William Drummond, 1931
Restoration: Hasbrouck-Hunderman, 1983; McClier Corporation, 1989–92

Nicknamed for the birds that roosted in the temporary City Hall that had occupied this site, the eleven-story Rookery combines structural and mechanical innovations with a sophisticated aesthetic. Designer John Wellborn Root, trained as an engineer, was challenged to support the enormous bulk of this building on Chicago's marshy soil. He devised a new foundation system, called "floating foundations," concrete rafts interleaved with iron rails for added strength. The architects, experimenting with steel-frame technology, employed a metal frame for the Quincy Court side of the building, but the rest of the Rookery uses traditional bearing-wall construction. The robust Romanesque exterior has a two-story rusticated granite base punctuated by glass and stone columns, a grand arched entry (note the two rooks), and intricate terra-cotta ornament. But the Rookery's interior is its glory: a two-story glass-roofed atrium supported by an iron frame, providing maximum light to interior offices while creating a dynamic spatial experience. Note the curving, cantilevered oriel staircase, with its carved Moorish details. Twenty years after the atrium's completion, Frank Lloyd Wright (1867–1959) modernized the space by replacing much of the delicate ironwork with gold-incised white marble.

Graham, Anderson, Probst and White
135 South LaSalle Street
1928–34

Located on the site of William Le Baron Jenney's Home Insurance Building (often considered the first skyscraper), the Field Building was an ambitious, speculative venture developed by the Marshall Field Estate trustees during the Great Depression. The modern, luxurious, million-square-foot office building was designed to offer first-class office space while symbolizing faith in Chicago's future. Designed by Alfred P. Shaw (1895–1970), the exterior is simple and elegant: four 22-story wings surround a central 43-story shaft sheathed in Indiana limestone. The shaft's skyward thrust is emphasized by recessed spandrels and soaring setbacks. The Clark and LaSalle Street entrances, connected by one of Chicago's few block-through arcades, are dressed with sleek Art Moderne motifs, such as stylized lettering and incised white bronze zigzags set in polished black granite. The Art Moderne style continues in the two-story lobby, where indirect lighting highlights distinctive nickel silver metalwork, high-speed elevators are monitored by the giant elevator indicator, and the main mail chute is cast in a bronze relief of the Field Building itself. Technologically advanced for its day, it was the last building built in the Loop until the construction of the Inland Steel building (see #29) twenty years later.

John Burgee with Philip Johnson
1983–7

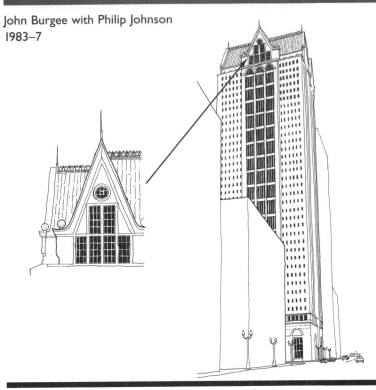

This 40-story office building of red granite was inspired by John Wellborn Root's 22-story Masonic Temple Building of 1890 that stood on the southwest corner of Randolph and State until it was destroyed in 1931. Like the Masonic Temple Building, 190 South LaSalle has arches that stretch up the facade, culminating in pairs of distinctive, two-story crested gables. A huge multi-use complex for its time, the Masonic Temple Building had a full-height atrium, a rooftop garden and promenade, and ten floors of shopping, restaurants, offices, and other facilities. As a speculative office building, 190 South LaSalle's programmatic requirements were simpler. However, its sumptuous gold-leaf barrel-vaulted lobby still recalls the grandeur of the past. The building exemplifies Postmodernism, a style or attitude that moves away from abstraction and toward reinterpreting representational forms, often drawing upon connections to the past. Although architect John Burgee (b. 1933) grew up in the Chicago area and practiced here before joining Philip Johnson (b. 1906) in New York, 190 South LaSalle is his first major office building completed in Chicago. By recalling a demolished historic building, it extends the memory of Root's work, while connecting itself to Chicago's remarkable design tradition.

Skidmore, Owings & Merrill
233 South Wacker Drive
1968–74; entrance addition, 1984–5
Renovation: DeStefano + Partners, 1992–3

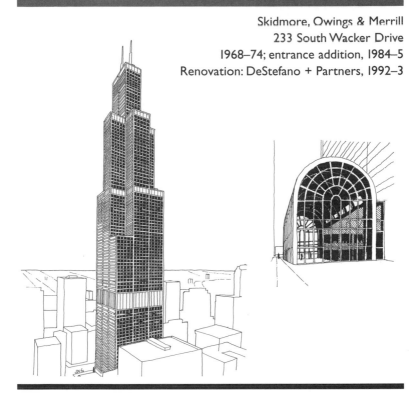

At 110 stories and 1,454 feet high, the Sears Tower is among the tallest buildings in the world. To ensure stability, a system of 75-foot-square structural tubes is used, to act as perimeter columns to brace the skyscraper against powerful wind forces. Nine of these huge tubes form the building's base. As the building rises, the number of tubes is reduced where setbacks occur: at the fiftieth, sixty-sixth, and ninetieth floors. Two tubes remain to support the tower, while steel columns comprising the building's frame serve to channel wind shear and gravity stress down to bedrock caissons. Design partner Bruce Graham (b. 1925) and engineer Fazlur Khan (1929–82) led the project team for this immense undertaking. It both symbolized Sears Roebuck and Company's position as the largest retailer in the world and consolidated the company's offices. With its dark angular silhouette, the Sears Tower soon became a Chicago icon, but it was forbidding at street level. Several years ago, Skidmore, Owings & Merrill returned to design a vaulted atrium as a friendlier entrance and to renovate the lobby. Recent work by DeStefano + Partners has created a more inviting lobby and better tourist access.

Skidmore, Owings and Merrill
227 West Monroe Street
1985–9

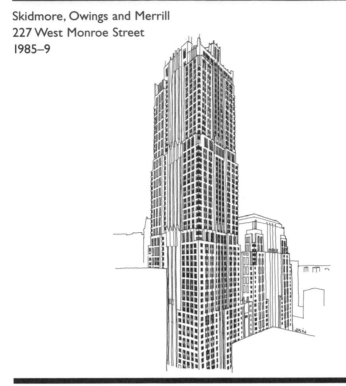

Architect Adrian Smith (b. 1944) sought to integrate the AT&T Corporate Center into the existing urban context by drawing upon the Art Moderne aesthetic of the 1920s, as seen in the Chicago Board of Trade (see #8) and the Field Building (see #12). Note the strong verticality of the AT&T Corporate Center's tripartite facade, with its recessed central plane, setbacks at the thirtieth, forty-fifth, and fifty-ninth floors, and stylized decorative details. The complex comprises two granite towers connected by an arcade from Monroe to Adams Street. The 60-story AT&T tower is polished red granite at the base, with lighter shades above, and its window spandrels are clad with 2,600 silkscreened dark-green aluminum panels. To relate such a large mass to the human scale, Smith placed a cornice line at the fifth story, which, with the Norway maple trees on the sidewalk, forms a kind of pedestrian canopy. The 4,000-square-foot lobby is one of the finest in the city; marble and fine woods are used to create intricate patterns. The second tower is 34 stories high and topped with a hipped roof. The complex creates an interesting dynamic and a sharp contrast to the Sears Tower nearby.

Murphy/Jahn
1992

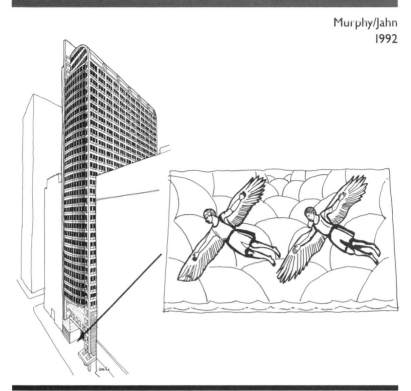

This 40-story mid-block building on an asymmetrical site presented several challenges to architect Helmut Jahn. For example, in order to provide maximum floorplate size, he placed all fixed elements in a side core of the building, a design not unlike that of the Inland Steel building (see #29); to enhance natural light and enlarge the view, he extended a curved glass bay over LaSalle Street, permitting views of the LaSalle Street canyon. In addition, penthouse offices are topped by the vaulting glass curved roof of the structure. The building's exterior skin is alternating bands of gray and white granite, a pattern repeated in the lobby floor. The focus of the lobby is artist Roger Brown's 20- by 50-foot mosaic of Daedalus, the mythical patron saint of architecture, who is shown escaping into the clouds with his son Icarus on wings fashioned of wax and feathers. On the ground floor, storefronts are suspended clear glass without vertical mullions, resulting in a transparent wall with a clear view of the interior lobby. Other Jahn designs in the Loop include One South Wacker Drive, the Xerox Centre (see #31), the Chicago Board of Trade addition (see #8), and the State of Illinois Center (see #20).

D. H. Burnham and Co. and Graham, Burnham and Company
111 West Washington Street
1912–3
Now known as the Chicago Title and Trust Building

Developed by the estate of Marshall Field and named after Field's birth-place, Conway, Massachusetts, this 21-story office building follows the pro-totype developed by the architectural firm D. H. Burnham and Co. at the turn of the century: a two-story glass atrium lobby, above which is a square open well to provide light and ventilation, and glazed white terra-cotta sheathing, reflecting Burnham's wish to "lighten up" commercial buildings in the Loop. Classical detailing also recalls the influence of the 1893 World's Columbian Exposition, where the Beaux Arts aesthetic dominated. Note the Conway Building's rounded corners (typical of many nineteenth-cen-tury Loop buildings), and its unaltered three-story rooftop colonnade and elaborate balustrade. Frederick H. Dinkelberg (c. 1869–1935) of D. H. Burnham's office is credited with this design; when Burnham died in 1912, his successor firm, Graham, Burnham and Company, completed the project. When the building was purchased in 1944, the new owner filled in the interior court to the height of six stories to create more offices.

Holabird and Roche
77 West Washington
1922–3
Formerly First Methodist-Episcopal Church,
now First United Methodist Church

The tallest church in the world, the First United Methodist Church sits at the base of a 21-story commercial office tower. The building's entrances are separated according to purpose: Washington Street for the offices, Clark Street to reach the 1,500-seat sanctuary. Above the office block is an eight-story Gothic spire; its additional weight is distributed by a complex system of girders and bracing. Within the spire is the Chapel in the Sky and a rectory for the minister. At 556 feet, the building was more than twice Chicago's height limit of the time: 260 feet. Fortunately, the City Council granted a waiver of the ordinance before the building was completed. This valuable site is located diagonally across from the original Courthouse Square, now the site of the City and County Building (see #19), and has been owned by the church since 1845; far smaller church buildings preceded the present edifice. Today's economic and development pressures have led some churches to realize the value of their air rights by building skyscrapers that tower above their steeples. However, Holabird and Roche's solution kept the church's position intact, for in their design the spire, not the office tower, is closer to the heavens.

Holabird and Roche
Block bounded by LaSalle, Clark, Randolph, and Washington Streets
County Building, 1907; City Hall, 1911

In 1831, the Illinois legislature created Cook County, established Chicago as the county seat, and designated this block for a county courthouse that was built four years later. In 1848, John Mills Van Osdel (1811–91) designed the first city offices above the public market, straddling State Street north of Randolph. City and county government functions were first joined on the courthouse site in another building designed by Van Osdel in 1853. Chicago's explosive economic growth soon required enlarged governmental facilities. After the Chicago fire of 1871, a massive City Hall/County Building designed by James Egan (1839–1914) was finally completed in 1885, but was demolished twenty years later for the present structure. Here, Holabird and Roche's use of classical elements on a monumental scale defines the eleven-story gray granite structure as a public building. Note, for example, the majestic colonnade of six-story Corinthian columns, massive piers, and the 24-foot-high entablature. On the interior, the lobby walls are faced in Botticino marble, as are the ceiling vaults and main corridors on the upper floors. This City and County Building has now served local government for nearly 90 years, a testament to its functionality and symbolic civic virtues.

Murphy/Jahn with Lester B. Knight and Associates
Bounded by Randolph, LaSalle, Lake, and Clark Streets
1979–85

Has a spaceship landed in the Loop? Helmut Jahn's 1,150,000-square-foot State of Illinois Center is a daring polychrome design that reinterprets the classical forms and grammar of monumental public buildings. In a city renowned for its skyscrapers, this low, seventeen-story building makes an impact with its cylindrical shape, playful details, and spectacular skylit rotunda. Occupying a full city block, the structure follows the city grid on three sides, but pulls back at the southeast corner to form a curved entrance. Note sculptor Jean Dubuffet's (1901–85) *Monument with Standing Beast* (1984). The glass and steel exterior is divided into three tiers by setbacks, while the surface juxtaposes silver and blue vertical stripes with horizontal salmon bands. Like a great round eye, a modern-day dome rises from the edge of the roof at a 45-degree angle. At the concourse level, a spiral-patterned marble and granite floor emphasizes the curving interior space. Free-standing glass elevators and escalators leading to state offices are placed at the edge of the 160-foot-diameter rotunda. Although it carries noise and dirt into work areas, the openness was meant to symbolize government accessibility.

C. F. Murphy Associates; Skidmore, Owings and Merrill; and Loebl Schlossman and Bennett

Bounded by Washington, Randolph, Dearborn, and Clark Streets

1965

Formerly Chicago Civic Center

Set on the north side of a great open plaza, the 31-story tower, designed by Jacques Brownson (b. 1923) of C. F. Murphy Associates, gives Chicago an extraordinary public space. The placement of the tower on the site opens the view to Holabird and Roche's Beaux Arts City and County Building (see #19), which provides a striking contrast to the Daley Center's structural grid of glass and steel. Yet they share the monumental proportions that mark public buildings in Chicago. For example, each of the Daley Center's three structural bays is 87 feet long and almost 48 feet wide, and the long spandrels are stretched across the facade like bridge girders. Note how the great rectangular columns, strongly rooted in the ground, become progressively thinner as they rise to the roof. The whole surface is integrated by the use of amber-tinted glass and Cor-Ten steel, which ages to a rich brown. Picasso's 50-foot-high sculpture is also of Cor-Ten steel and was the artist's gift to the city of Chicago. A modern sphinx, it hears the city at its feet: farmers' markets, political rallies, summertime music, and the latest deal.

Rapp and Rapp
175 North State Street
1921

The Chicago Theatre marquee is a Loop landmark and a symbol of the city. Note the City of Chicago's insignia: an encircled "Y," representing the three branches of the Chicago River. Built when cinema design was evolving from simple storefront nickelodeons showing silent pictures to the flamboyant movie theaters of the later 1920s, the 4,000-seat Chicago Theatre was one of the earliest and largest movie palaces constructed in America and one of the few of its kind extant. The decorative theme was French, not surprising for a city that compared itself to Paris in the Burnham Plan of 1909. The Arc de Triomphe inspired the Chicago Theatre's exterior facade on State Street, the Grand Lobby was modeled after J. H. Mansart's chapel at Versailles, and Louis XIV-style furnishings were placed throughout. Music was provided by the Chicago Theatre Symphony Orchestra and by the famous Chicago Theatre Grande Wurlitzer pipe organ, restored in 1970. Theater design requires an understanding of engineering, acoustics, and interior decoration. Rapp and Rapp became highly successful specialists in this field. Their work includes the Tivoli, Oriental, and Uptown theaters in Chicago, as well as the Times Square and Brooklyn Paramount in New York City.

John Mills Van Osdel
177–91 North State Street
1872

The Page Brothers Building is remarkable for its cast-iron facade, one of two remaining in Chicago's Loop. The former site of the City Hotel, which had been destroyed in the 1871 Chicago fire, this property was developed as a 70-foot-long store and warehouse that was partitioned by brick firewalls into three separate sections for different tenants. The wholesale leather firm of Page Brothers & Company occupied the corner section. The Page Brothers Building was designed by John Mills Van Osdel, who came to Chicago in 1837 to supervise the building of Mayor William B. Ogden's residence. In 1844, he established Chicago's first architectural practice, which provided many noteworthy structures for the booming young city—grain elevators, the first City Hall, and an elegant Palmer House Hotel. Van Osdel was also responsible for introducing cast-iron architecture to Chicago prior to the Civil War. For this building, he ordered the facade from Daniel D. Badger's Architectural Iron Works in New York. Since the strength of cast iron allowed a greater proportion of glass to solid wall, more natural light was available for interior working or selling space. Further, cast iron's plasticity allowed it to be cast into a variety of ornamental shapes, providing stylish exteriors for competitive enterprises.

Tigerman Fugman McCurry
60 East Lake Street
1984–6

Clever and functional, the facade of this twelve-story parking garage is designed to look like the front of an automobile. The first two stories are retail and office space, with a SelfPark "license plate" in the middle marking the mezzanine level. The parking garage itself is indicated by a center metal grille with turquoise baked-enamel panels from a 1957 Chevrolet color chart. Awnings painted to look like tire treads flank the entrance; above them, near the top of the building, are two acrylic sky-lights placed to resemble car headlights. The composition is crowned by a draped, helmeted figure resembling a hood ornament. Is he shaking his fist at the world around him or proclaiming the triumph of good design? Perhaps only architect Stanley Tigerman (b. 1930) knows. Born in Chicago, he was trained at the Massachusetts Institute of Technology and the Yale School of Architecture and was Dean of the School of Architecture at the University of Illinois at Chicago before forming Archeworks, a new design school in Chicago. Tigerman's early designs were influenced primarily by the work of Mies van der Rohe, and his career reflects a continuing exploration of modern American values, sometimes with an engaging sense of humor.

D. H. Burnham and Co.; Graham, Burnham and Company
Block bounded by Wabash, Washington, State, and Randolph Streets
1892, 1902, 1906, 1907, 1914

"Meet me under the clock," Chicagoans say, and they mean, of course, at the Marshall Field and Company store. As the flagship operations of Chicago's legendary retailer, this store is synonymous with State Street shopping. Its oldest section, at Wabash and Washington Streets, resembles an Italian Renaissance palazzo and was completed a year before the World's Columbian Exposition of 1893. However, the main sections of the Marshall Field store, on State Street, completed between 1902 and 1907, reflect the influence of the Beaux Arts classicism featured at the 1893 Fair. The facade is divided into a three-story base, a mid-section of Ionic columns placed between Chicago-style windows, and a classically detailed entablature. The main entrance is marked by four three-story-high columns, emphasizing the building's dignity and formality. The interior has two multi-story atria. At the north end, colorful Louis Comfort Tiffany mosaics face the dome; to the south, classical decorative elements are used with a restrained palette. This design became a prototype for department stores in the United States and abroad. Among the firm's notable retail commissions were Selfridge's (1906) in London, Wanamaker's (1903) and Gimbel's (1909) in New York, and Filene's (1912) in Boston.

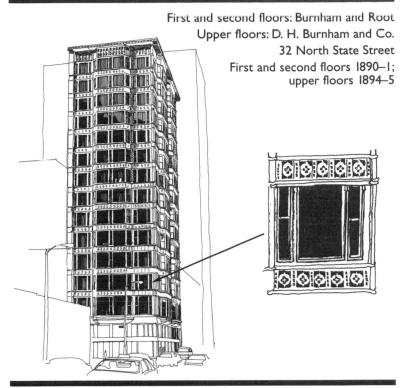

First and second floors: Burnham and Root
Upper floors: D. H. Burnham and Co.
32 North State Street
First and second floors 1890–1;
upper floors 1894–5

The Reliance Building is considered the ultimate skeleton frame-and-glass representative of the Chicago School of Architecture. At the time of its construction, its Chicago windows were the largest yet built relative to the building's frame, which itself is thin and light. Only the gothically decorated white terra-cotta tiles connect it to an older tradition. The Reliance Building is also notable for its colorful construction history. The site was acquired in 1882 by William Ellery Hale, a prosperous hydraulic elevator manufacturer and friend to Daniel Burnham. Unfortunately his new property could not be redeveloped immediately since it was encumbered by leases expiring at different dates: the lease on the lower two floors expired in May 1890, but the lease on the upper three lasted until 1894. How to maximize investment? John Root's solution was to demolish and reconstruct the lower floors, while supporting the rest of the existing building on huge jacks. The lower floors were then leased to Carson Pirie Scott and Company, while the upper-floor tenants climbed stairs to go about their business. When the leases on the upper floors expired, those floors were replaced with this extraordinary tower by Charles Atwood, who had become Burnham's chief designer after Root's death in 1891.

Louis H. Sullivan
1 South State Street
1899, 1903–4
Five bays on State Street: D. H. Burnham and Co., 1906
Three bays on State Street: Holabird and Root, 1960–1
Renovation of rotunda and exterior ornament: John Vinci Associates, 1979
Formerly the Schlesinger
and Mayer Store

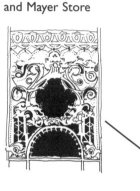

Brilliant, visionary, idiosyncratic architect Louis Sullivan (1856–1924) designed this department store at the height of his creative powers. Originally, it was only nine stories high and three bays wide, fronting on Madison Street. Four years later, Sullivan took full advantage of the opportunity to expand the store, now owned by Carson Pirie Scott and Company, to twelve stories that wrap around the crucial corner to State Street, Chicago's retail center. Inside, the spatial organization is functional, efficient, and filled with light. On the exterior, a restrained facade is wedded to extraordinary street-level ornament. Sullivan organized the building in three parts: a simple cornice at top; a midsection, faced in white terra cotta and set with wide Chicago windows, that reveals the underlying structure; and a two-story base with dark, intricate cast-iron ornament that contrasts with the pale facade. In the cartouches framing the doors and display windows, Sullivan gave expression to his theory of natural forms; densely intertwined wreaths create a distinctive entrance that became emblematic of the store in many advertisements. Look for Sullivan's initials, LHS, superimposed on each other at the base of the arches over the State and Madison entrance doors.

Holabird and Roche
7 West Madison Street
1903–4

The fifteen-story Chicago Building, with its dark brown terra-cotta facade, is a Chicago School of Architecture gem, displaying all the elements central to the style. The building is divided into a base, thirteen-story shaft, and still intact cornice; its facade expresses the underlying steel frame. Further, it uses two kinds of windows characteristic to Chicago: the projecting bay along narrow Madison Street, which catches available light from three sides, and on wide State Street the flat expanse of a fixed pane flanked on both sides by movable sash windows. Like Holabird and Roche's earlier Marquette Building (see #32), corners are reinforced to emphasize the edge of the block. Construction of the Chicago Building was financed through the creation of the Chicago Savings Bank, which was located in the building until 1913. William Holabird (1854–1923) and Martin Roche (1853–1927) met in the offices of engineer William Le Baron Jenney. Holabird and Roche established their firm in 1883, and it soon became one of Chicago's most successful practices, noted for its clarity of organization and original solutions to tall office building design. Today that tradition is continued by the successor firm Holabird and Root.

Skidmore, Owings & Merrill
30 West Monroe Street
1954–8

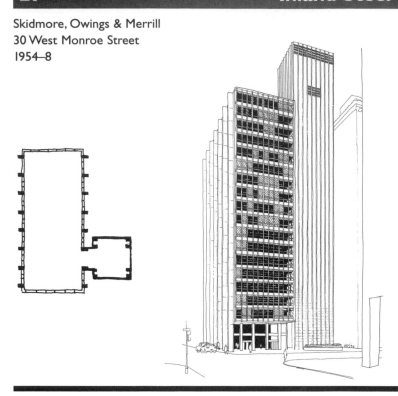

The gleaming nineteen-story Inland Steel building was the first commercial office tower to rise in the Loop after the Great Depression and World War II, and the first downtown Chicago project for Skidmore, Owings & Merrill, founded in 1936. Walter Netsch (b. 1920) did the initial design work for the building in 1954; when Netsch took on another assignment, Bruce Graham assumed the project. It was Graham's first major commission, and marks the beginning of a distinguished career that includes the John Hancock Center (1970), Sears Tower (see #14), and One Magnificent Mile (1983). Inland Steel was the prototype of many structural features and commercial amenities that are now commonplace. It was, for instance, the first major building erected on steel pilings rather than concrete caissons; it has a basement parking garage and central air-conditioning. The seven columns located on both its west (Dearborn) and east faces are the building's most striking feature: connected by 60-foot girders, these columns support the entire weight of the building and provide clear-span interior spaces. A separate 25-story service tower to the east, also clad in stainless steel, contains elevators, mechanical systems, and other core facilities, giving the offices maximum layout flexibility.

C. F. Murphy Associates, with The Perkins and Will Partnership
Madison Street between Dearborn and Clark Streets
1964–9

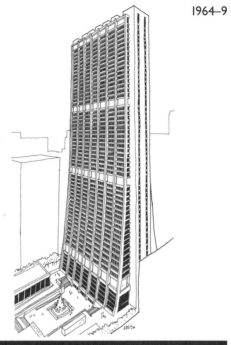

The dramatic, graceful inward curve of this 60-story monochromatic buff granite building is functional as well as aesthetic. Since banking public facilities require ample space, they were placed in the building's broad base. Above this two-story lobby, conventional offices house bank employees and other tenants. Elevators are placed at the building's ends to create open floor plans. The rooftop houses a parade of penthouses containing mechanical systems that form a distinctive denticulated silhouette. In 1972, D. H. Burnham and Co.'s 1896 First National Bank Building at the corner of Monroe and Dearborn was demolished to create a sunken plaza from Dearborn to Clark Streets along Monroe Street. This popular plaza is one of three created between Dearborn and Clark Streets during the 1960s to relieve the density of the Loop: to the north is Richard J. Daley Center (see #21) and to the south is Mies van der Rohe's Federal Center (see #33). Note Marc Chagall's mosaic, *The Four Seasons*, the artist's gift to the city of Chicago. Fourteen feet high, ten feet wide, and seventy feet in length, it depicts imagined Chicago scenes.

C. F. Murphy Associates
55 West Monroe
1977–80

Stretched like a striped silver skin around the corner of Dearborn and Monroe, the 40-story, 800,000-square-foot Xerox Centre is a shining, elegant high-rise in the heart of the Loop. Clad in white-painted aluminum and reflective glass, the walls seem to weave behind the corner tower piece, an illusion created by the different horizontal window levels and the swept-back roof banding. At the street level, diagonal sidewalk paving creates a pattern; on the rooftop, angled striping, visible from taller skyscrapers, repeats this design device. Jahn was born in Germany and received his early training there. At the age of 26, he came to Chicago to study at the Illinois Institute of Technology, where Mies van der Rohe had taught the principles of modern architecture for many years. Historians suggest that Jahn was inspired by Louis Sullivan's Carson Pirie Scott and Company department store (see #27) a block away or by Expressionist Erich Mendelsohn's Schocken Department Store (1928) in Germany. Whatever the influences, Jahn has a technical virtuosity all his own, integrating historic references into expressive forms and materials with confidence, energy, and power.

Holabird and Roche
140 South Dearborn Street
1893–5
Renovation: Holabird and Root
1979–81

The Marquette Building is a masterpiece of early commercial high-rise architecture. Its exterior grid expresses the underlying skeleton frame, while its wide, flat windows, framed at each side by movable sash, are an early example of the "Chicago window." Yet there is subtlety in this apparent simplicity. The tripartite facade is composed of a two-story base with classically derived terra-cotta ornament, such as meander and acanthus leaves; a powerful twelve-story midsection where vertical piers rise smoothly to the roofline and spandrels are recessed; and a two-story decorative cornice, now replaced by a plain seventeenth floor. Corner bays are slightly enlarged and emphasized by horizontal coursing. Owen Aldis, Chicago agent for Boston developers Peter and Shepherd Brooks, translated Marquette's journal; his interest in the Northwest Territory's exploration is evident in the decoration of this building, named in Marquette's honor. Bronze bas-reliefs depicting scenes from the life of Marquette enliven the Dearborn Street entrance; a balcony frieze in the rotunda portrays the discovery of the Northwest in mother-of-pearl and favrile-glass panels designed by J. A. Holzer of Tiffany Glass; and Edward Kemeys' bronze heads of Indians and French explorers top the sixteen elevator doors.

Ludwig Mies van der Rohe with Schmidt, Garden, and Erikson;
C. F. Murphy Associates; and A. Epstein and Sons
Dearborn Street between Jackson Boulevard and Adams Street
1959–75

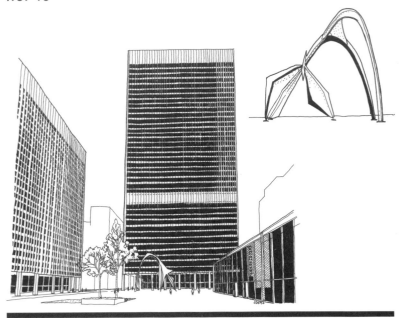

The Federal Center gave Mies van der Rohe (1886–1969) the opportunity
to plan a modern complex in Chicago's Loop amid such Chicago School
masterpieces as the Monadnock and Marquette Buildings (see #6 and #32).
The three government buildings that comprise the Federal Center all face
a large plaza dominated by *Flamingo*, a red metal stabile created by noted
sculptor Alexander Calder (1898–1976). The buildings share common
lobby heights, glass and steel exteriors, and light-gray granite floors. The
30-story Everett McKinley Dirksen Building (1964), a federal courthouse
and office building, was the first completed. It stands east of the plaza, at
230 South Dearborn Street. After Mies died in 1969, architects Gene
Summers (b. 1923) and Bruno Conterato (1920–95) completed the
remaining two buildings of the project: the single-story Post Office at the
southwest corner of Clark and Adams and the 43-story John C. Kluczynski
Office Tower (both 1975). This complex replaced Henry Ives Cobb's
(1859–1931) full-block, classical Federal Building (1905). In 1991, a fourth federal structure, the Ralph H. Metcalfe Building, was completed at 77 West
Jackson Boulevard. Designed by Mies' successor firm, Fujikawa Johnson and
Associates, its form and exterior are consistent with the existing complex.

Palmer Building: C. M. Palmer
Stone Building: unknown
15–27 West Adams Street
1872 (both)
Formerly known as the Stone and Palmer Buildings

These extraordinary remnants of Chicago history were built immediately after the devastating 1871 fire, in what was then the fringe of the commercial district. They are typical of pre- as well as post-fire construction. Although both buildings were designed in the Italianate style, with rows of arched windows and symmetrical facades, each has unique features. The three-story Stone Building, clad in Cleveland sandstone, is divided into three sections marked by piers articulating the fire wall behind the facade. The center bifora window, a double-arched opening within a larger arched frame, is the building's dominant feature. Incised lines on the exterior provide illusionary joints between regular courses of ashlar-faced rusticated blocks and reinforce the building's surface regularity. The Stone Building's third story was a public meeting hall, the last surviving downtown example of a once common building usage. To the west, the Palmer Building was developed by real estate tycoon Potter Palmer (1826–1902) as part of his extensive property holdings in the Loop. It is one of only two remaining cast-iron-front buildings in Chicago (see #23). Such fashionable facades were prefabricated, bolted together on site, and fastened into the load-bearing masonry walls.

Holabird and Roche
542 South Dearborn Street
1889–91
Renovation: Booth/Hansen & Associates
1985

Named for the great Ottawa Indian chief, Pontiac, who led the 1763–4 uprising against the British in the Great Lakes region, this fourteen-story brick and terra-cotta building is located in "Printing House Row." It was originally planned for light industrial use. However, by completion of construction, the real estate market had changed, so it was leased for office space instead. One of the first skeleton-frame buildings, its facade is notable for the broad expanses of glass and the projecting bays that capture as much light and air as possible in what was a sooty, noisy section of the city. The two lower stories, still unaltered, are tied together by thin, limestone-clad piers with elegant ornamental capitals. Above them are the richly detailed terra-cotta soffits of the bay windows. The Pontiac Building's cornice is still intact, as are many of its interior doors and hardware. The oldest surviving example of Holabird and Roche's work, this building reflects the interplay between solid and void made possible by the skeleton frame and more fully exploited in their later work, including the Monadnock and Marquette Buildings (see #6 and #32).

George C. Nimmons
720–36 South Dearborn Street
1912

This straightforward, thirteen-story red brick loft building was constructed with heavy timbers and reinforced concrete floors to support heavy printing presses and other machinery. Located on "Printing House Row," it is distinguished by the polychrome terra-cotta panels on its facade, which illustrate the history of printing. Over the entrance a mural depicts the printing of the first book with movable type, the Gutenberg Bible. Spandrels contain geometric patterns, and the terra-cotta decoration continues to the top of the building, where a sunburst motif lies at the center of the roofline gable. The facade is composed of a base with nine two-story tapering piers outlined with white terra cotta; a shaft of nine unornamented piers rising from the second to the ninth floors; and a two-story upper section that repeats the tapering piers design. George C. Nimmons (1865–1940) was associated with the Prairie School of architecture that flourished from the turn of the century until World War I. Best known for his commercial work, Nimmons also designed the Reid, Murdoch and Company headquarters on the Chicago River (1913–4) and, in partnership with William K. Fellows, the Sears Roebuck and Company headquarters complex (1904) on West Arthington Street at Homan Avenue.

Cyrus W. Eidlitz
47 West Polk Street, at the foot of Dearborn Street
1883–5
Formerly the Chicago and Western
Indiana Railway Station

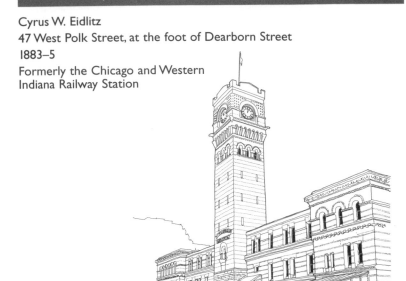

Chicago's last surviving nineteenth-century railroad station, the Dearborn Street Station was developed by a consortium of five railroad companies, headed by the Chicago and Western Indiana line, to secure entry into the city of Chicago. The new station was ensured a prominent site at the foot of Dearborn Street when the city extended the street southward from Van Buren to Polk Street in 1881. Designed by New York architect Cyrus Eidlitz (1853–1921), the Romanesque revival building has a base of pink rusticated granite and walls of red pressed brick with deep red terra-cotta details. Originally, the headhouse had gable roofs of vertically striated slate, and the clocktower was capped with a steeply pitched roof as well, but these were destroyed in a 1922 fire. Construction of this important station fostered development of the surrounding land, where the printing industry of the Midwest concentrated around the explosive growth of mail-order catalogs from companies such as Sears Roebuck and Montgomery Ward. After passenger operations ceased in 1971, Dearborn Street Station was renovated as office and retail space and the vast railroad yards behind the station were replaced with small-scale residential development.

Graham, Anderson, Probst and White
210 South Canal Street
1916–25

The Union Station complex combines Beaux Arts grandeur with sophisticated planning, engineering, and railroad technology. It was expected to
provide the major link between the Loop, suburban commuting networks,
and the planned but never realized Civic Center, which would have been
to the west on Congress Street. When completed, it could handle up to
720 trains a day because its double stub-end plan allows trains to move
in either direction at either end. The complex was organized as two distinct buildings, the headhouse, or waiting room, and the smaller Concourse
Building facing the Chicago River (demolished in 1969); between them was
a passageway where ticket offices and baggage facilities were located. From
the outside, the waiting room appears as a conventional eight-story
office building, but the 100- by 269-foot interior, with its glass skylight vault,
grand perimeter Corinthian columns, and Roman travertine walls, is a monumental space, built when people who traveled did so by rail, and terminals
had enormous symbolic power. Architect Peirce Anderson (1870–1936)
is credited with the design of Union Station. Anderson, who trained at
Harvard and the Ecole des Beaux Arts, became Daniel Burnham's chief
designer in 1898. He also designed Union Station in Washington, D.C.

Murphy/Jahn
500 West Madison Street
1979–87

The Northwestern Atrium, which replaced the Beaux Arts masonry Chicago and NorthWestern Terminal designed by Frost and Granger in 1911, is a 37-story, 1.6-million-square-foot glass and aluminum complex. The new building evokes the spatial grandeur of nineteenth-century train stations while dealing with the challenge of multi-use space and levels. Both commuters and tenants enter a 90-foot-high skylit retail gallery that extends the entire length of the facade. Ground-level escalators lead to a 110-foot-high atrium at train level; a second escalator bank leads to the office lobby above. On the exterior, dark-blue enameled aluminum ribbons emphasize the building's verticality; the Art Deco style is suggested by the streamlined horizontal glass curves cascading down the tripartite facade, with its central rounded tower. Note also how the building's Madison Street silhouette echoes that of Riverside Plaza, which was completed in 1929. Northwestern Atrium's concentric arched entry recalls those of Chicago's demolished Transportation and Stock Exchange Buildings, both designed by noted architect Louis Sullivan in the late nineteenth century. This complex is a fine example of architect Helmut Jahn's work, which integrates curving, muscular, colorful forms with structural expressiveness.

John Alexander Low Waddell
El stations: A. M. Hedley, consulting architect
Lake Street to Wabash Avenue to Van Buren Street to Wells Street
1892–1908

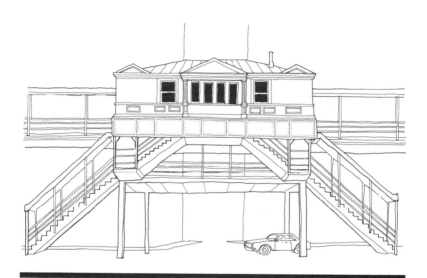

The Loop's elevated train is a powerful symbol of the connections between commerce, transportation, land values, politics, and emerging technology that existed in turn-of-the-century Chicago. Explosive economic growth concentrated in Chicago's small business district created very congested streets, so an alternative was sought to the slow, street-running cable cars. (The cable cars' turnabouts along Lake, Wabash, Madison, and State had created the first "loop" in 1882.) John Alexander Low Waddell (1854–1938) designed a two-track railroad running on steel trestle bents with open-webbed trusses or riveted plate girders carried on columns 70 feet apart. It was built between 1892 and 1908 by various independent companies, beginning with the Chicago and South Side Rapid Transit Railroad, which created its first line in 1892 to transport passengers to the World's Columbian Exposition of 1893. This was followed by the Lake Street line (1893); the Metropolitan West Side Elevated Railroad (1895), which was the first electrically powered line; and the Union Elevated Railway (1897), built by entrepreneur Charles T. Yerkes to connect these lines in a "Loop." In 1900, the Northwestern Elevated (Ravenswood line) was added. In 1924, these lines were consolidated as the Chicago Rapid Transit Company.

The Riverfront

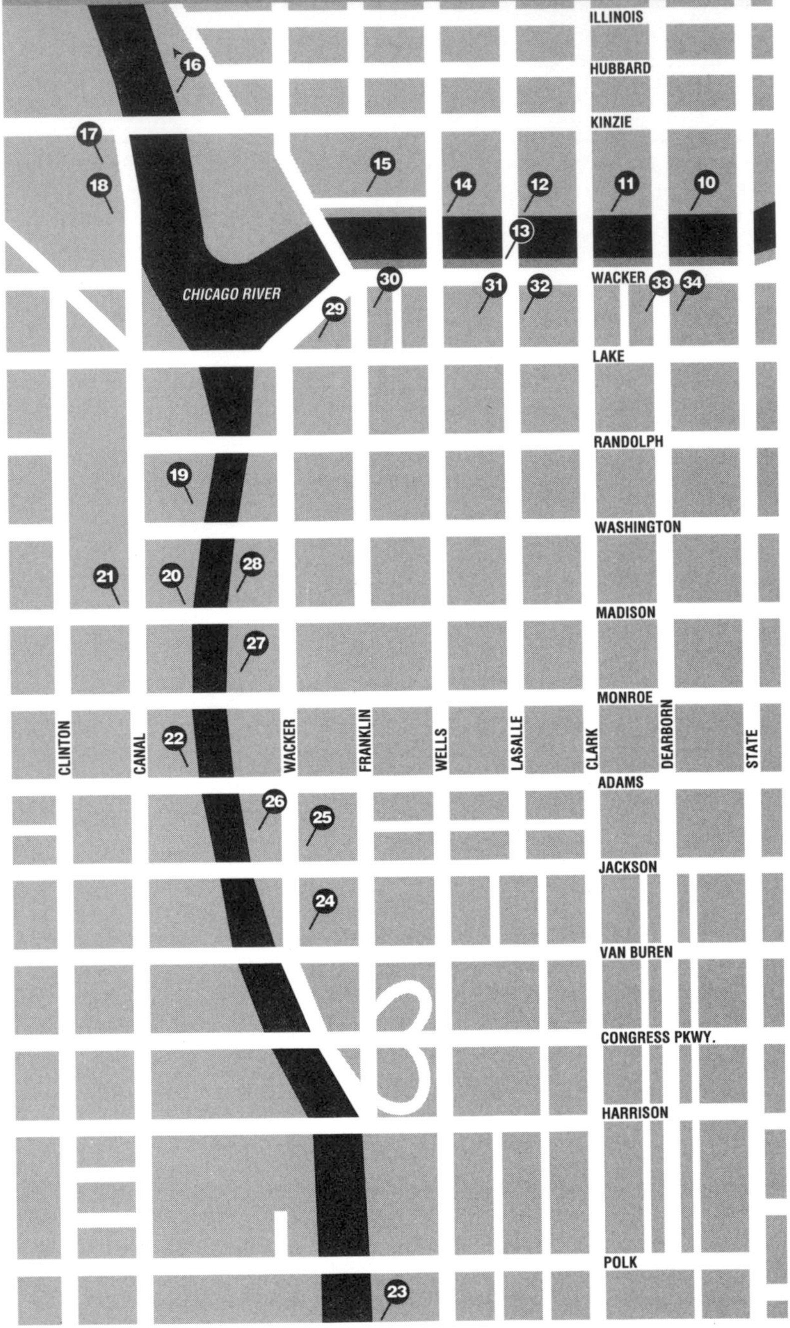

ILLINOIS
HUBBARD
KINZIE
WACKER
LAKE
RANDOLPH
WASHINGTON
MADISON
MONROE
ADAMS
JACKSON
VAN BUREN
CONGRESS PKWY.
HARRISON
POLK
CLINTON
CANAL
WACKER
FRANKLIN
WELLS
LASALLE
CLARK
DEARBORN
STATE
CHICAGO RIVER
10
11
12
13
14
15
16
17
18
19
20
21
22
23
24
25
26
27
28
29
30
31
32
33
34

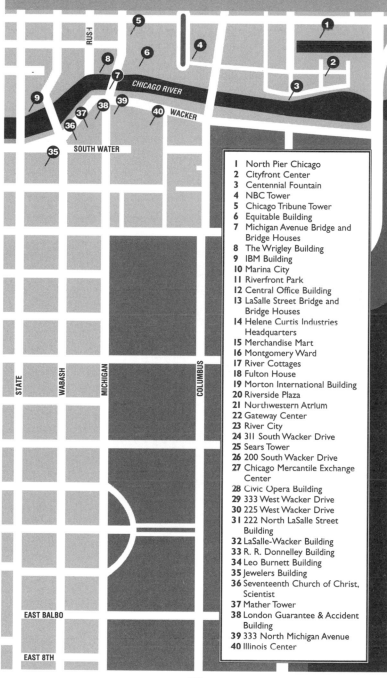

1 North Pier Chicago
2 Cityfront Center
3 Centennial Fountain
4 NBC Tower
5 Chicago Tribune Tower
6 Equitable Building
7 Michigan Avenue Bridge and Bridge Houses
8 The Wrigley Building
9 IBM Building
10 Marina City
11 Riverfront Park
12 Central Office Building
13 LaSalle Street Bridge and Bridge Houses
14 Helene Curtis Industries Headquarters
15 Merchandise Mart
16 Montgomery Ward
17 River Cottages
18 Fulton House
19 Morton International Building
20 Riverside Plaza
21 Northwestern Atrium
22 Gateway Center
23 River City
24 311 South Wacker Drive
25 Sears Tower
26 200 South Wacker Drive
27 Chicago Mercantile Exchange Center
28 Civic Opera Building
29 333 West Wacker Drive
30 225 West Wacker Drive
31 222 North LaSalle Street Building
32 LaSalle-Wacker Building
33 R. R. Donnelley Building
34 Leo Burnett Building
35 Jewelers Building
36 Seventeenth Church of Christ, Scientist
37 Mather Tower
38 London Guarantee & Accident Building
39 333 North Michigan Avenue
40 Illinois Center

Christian A. Eckstorm
Cityfront Center adjacent to Ogden Slip, 435 East Illinois Street
1905–20
Adaptive reuse: Booth/Hansen & Associates, 1986–8
Formerly Pugh Warehouse

Work on the Pugh Warehouse, named for developer James Andrew Pugh and designed by Christian Albert Eckstorm, began in 1905. Sections were gradually added, until by 1920 it stretched 1,663 feet eastward to the shore of Lake Michigan. Originally, it was the home of numerous manufacturers who displayed their products for the wholesale market. Later, after the larger Merchandise and Furniture Marts were built in the 1920s, it became a storage warehouse. Its location on protected Ogden Slip adjacent to the Chicago River and the lakefront allowed merchandise to be shipped easily by boat or by the rail lines that extended to the slip from the west. North Pier was part of an area of low-rise warehouses that stored lumber, grain, paper, and candy products. Today, this historic brick structure has been imaginatively adapted to new uses as a retail, office, dining, and recreational center To create greater accessibility and better views, architect Laurence Booth (b. 1936) designed two three-story glass galleries along the waterside. Their simple, rectangular lines recall the functional form of the warehouse itself.

1984 master plan: Cooper Eckstut Associates (now Cooper Robertson & Partners) with Skidmore, Owings & Merrill

1985 plan for The Chicago Dock & Canal Trust parcel: Lohan Associates

1985 plan for the Equitable Life Assurance Society of the United States parcel: Skidmore, Owings & Merrill

60 acres bordered by Grand Avenue (north), the Chicago River (south), Lake Shore Drive (east), and Michigan Avenue (west).

Begun in 1985

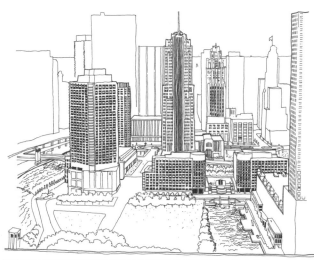

In 1857, Chicago's first Mayor, William B. Ogden, formed The Chicago Dock and Canal Company (now Trust) to own and develop property on the north bank of the Chicago River at the river's mouth. The area was developed first as a warehouse district, but as harbor traffic declined, Chicago Dock sought improved uses for this large site, and from 1983 to 1985 formed a joint venture with the Equitable Life Assurance Society to create a dynamic, mixed-use neighborhood that would also celebrate its important location. The result is Cityfront Center. Its master plan was developed by a two-firm architectural team in consultation with the Chicago Department of Planning. This Planned Unit Development pro-vides for 13.5 million square feet of office space, 5 million of residential use, half a million of retail facilities, and 4,000 hotel rooms. Projects completed to date include North Pier Chicago, the Centennial Fountain, and the NBC Tower (see #1, #3, and #4). Cityfront Center continues the grid of Chicago's existing streets, providing generous public spaces as well as riverfront access. This development is now a project directed by two separate entities: Chicago Dock directs the development of land east of Columbus Drive, while Equitable is responsible for the land west of it.

Lohan Associates
Cityfront Center at the McClurg Court Esplanade
1989

The Centennial Fountain commemorates the founding of the Metropolitan Water Reclamation District in 1889, the authority that was responsible for reversing the course of the Chicago River and today manages Chicago area water treatment. Before 1900, the Chicago River carried waste directly to Lake Michigan, the source of the city's drinking water. Periodic cholera epidemics threatened the population's health until the Sanitary and Ship Canal (1892–1900) was completed. Since the new canal bed was lower than that of the Chicago River, simple gravity diverted the river flow into the canal and away from the lake. Architect Dirk Lohan's (b. 1938) fountain design mirrors the divided flow of the water at the mouth of the river. The eastern half of the fountain symbolizes the river's connection to Lake Michigan and through the Great Lakes to the Atlantic Ocean, while the western half represents river's flow to the Des Plaines and Mississippi Rivers, then into the Gulf of Mexico. From the fountain's collecting pool, the water funnels into a cannon that projects a dramatic 80-foot-high water arch across the 222-foot-wide Chicago River to the opposite bank.

NBC Tower

Skidmore, Owings & Merrill
200 East Illinois Street
1985–9

Architect Adrian Smith's (b. 1944) NBC Tower was the first new building completed in Cityfront Center, the 60-acre multi-use development bordered by the Chicago River to the south. NBC Tower not only meets the guidelines set forth by Cityfront Center's Master Plan for materials and scale but also gracefully evokes the past. For example, NBC's soaring verticality, sleek setbacks, and masonry exterior recall the 333 North Michigan Avenue building across the river, while its load-bearing buttresses reference those of the nearby Tribune Tower (see #5). Here, the facade is articulated by rough-cut limestone piers alternating with coated precast spandrels finished to resemble terra cotta. The east and west entrances are detailed with intricate bronze metalwork and are further emphasized by a central bowed window that extends the entire height of the building and culminates in a spire facing Michigan Avenue. An adjacent four-story broadcasting studio continues the rhythm of the tower base elements and is connected to the tower by an interior lobby. This sensitive handling of form, materials, and site results in a romantic addition to the Chicago skyline.

Tower, Hood and Howells; printing plant, Jarvis Hunt (1859–1941)
435 North Michigan Avenue
Tower, 1922–5; printing plant, 1916–20

In 1922, the Chicago Tribune announced what became one of the twentieth century's most famous architectural competitions: $100,000 in prize money to design its new headquarters on a site near the just-completed Michigan Avenue Bridge and adjacent to the Tribune's new printing plant on the Chicago River, where the waterway facilitated shipment of newsprint and other operations. The 264 competition entries from around the world, included a fascinating range of designs for "the world's most beautiful office building." The winning entry, by Raymond Hood and John Mead Howells of New York, dresses a plain limestone shaft with the gargoyle gutters and flamboyant flying buttresses of France's great Gothic cathedrals. The grand arched entry and surrounding allegorical figures are impressive, but the tower steals the scene: a crown of open tracery that remains as visible and photogenic today as it was in 1922. Ironically, the contest's most influential entry may not have been the winner, but Finnish architect Eliel Saarinen's second-place design. Its strongly rooted and elegantly set-back mass helped define the skyscraper form for the rest of the century. Hood himself referred to it in his later designs in New York for the Daily News Building and Rockefeller Center complex.

Skidmore, Owings & Merrill
401 North Michigan Avenue
1962–5

On this site, pioneer Jean Baptiste du Sable, Chicago's first permanent settler, built his cabin. Now a 35-story office tower of glazed bronze solar glass with an aluminum curtain wall rises, recalling the structurally expressive style of noted architect Ludwig Mies van der Rohe (1886–1969). This aesthetic was often used by Skidmore, Owings & Merrill in its commercial high-rise designs. Here design partner Bruce Graham (b. 1925) used granite spandrels to mark the floors, while slender vertical piers containing circular pipes divide the windows into sets of four. This pattern gives the facade a subtle rhythm, enhanced when the Chicago River is reflected in the glass. The Chicago Tribune sold the land to the Equitable Life Assurance Society on condition that the new structure be no taller than the Tribune Tower and that, set back from Michigan Avenue, it not obstruct the Tribune's views. Pioneer Court, a plaza connecting the two buildings, is often used for summertime art exhibitions; via a sweeping spiral staircase, it also provides public access to the riverbank below. Such access was an amenity envisioned in the 1909 Plan of Chicago by architects Daniel Burnham and Edward Bennett.

7 Michigan Avenue Bridge and Bridge Houses

Edward H. Bennett, architect; Thomas Pihlfeldt, engineer of bridges; Hugh Young, engineer of bridge design; Henry Herring and J. E. Fraser, sculptors
Michigan Avenue and the Chicago River
1918–20; pylon sculptures, 1928

The Michigan Avenue Bridge blended the Beaux Arts aesthetics of Daniel Burnham's 1909 Plan of Chicago with the sophisticated engineering necessary to solve one of Chicago's worst transportation problems. Before 1920, when Michigan Avenue still ended at the river, nearly half of Chicago's north-south traffic converged at the old Rush Street swing bridge, which was also among the first bridges encountered by ships entering from the lake. To ease the resulting congestion, Chicago engineers perfected a bridge type in which leaves divide, rotate around a trunnion pin, and return to their fixed positions. The Michigan Avenue Bridge was their masterpiece: the world's first double-leaf, double-deck trunnion bascule bridge, capable of handling two levels of traffic and still clearing the channel in under 60 seconds. Much of Burnham's grand, classical design, modeled after the Seine bridges of Paris, was implemented after Burnham's death by Edward Bennett (1874–1954), consultant to the Chicago Plan Commission. Bennett's four limestone bridge houses create a monumental approach to this important crossing, while commemorative sculptures by J. E. Fraser and Henry Herring mark the historic location, spanning the sites of Fort Dearborn and Chicago's first pioneer homesteads.

Graham, Anderson, Probst and White
410 North Michigan Avenue
1919–22 (south tower); 1924–5 (north tower)

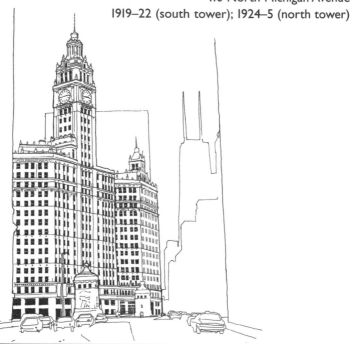

The Wrigley Building may be Chicago's favorite landmark. Its gleaming white facade and gently curving entrance plaza convey a bright, welcoming feeling; most familiar of all is the eleven-story clocktower, inspired by the Giralda Tower in Seville, Spain, which has also been spotlit at night from the outset. The building was developed by William Wrigley, founder of the chewing gum company, and remains the Wrigley Company headquarters today. As the first building completed north of the Chicago River on the newly extended Michigan Avenue, it initiated the area's redevelopment from a dingy warehouse district to a desirable commercial address. A second building was added to the north in 1925, and is connected to the first at the lobby and by an upper-level skywalk. Both are sheathed in terra cotta, a material popular both for its decorative potential, and for its fire-proofing ability, not underestimated in a city leveled by fire just 50 years before. To encourage public access to the Chicago River, a monumental staircase was designed that leads from the entrance plaza to a riverside landing where tour boats dock in the summertime.

Ludwig Mies van der Rohe with C. F. Murphy Associates
330 North Wabash Avenue, between Wabash and State on the
Chicago River
1969–71

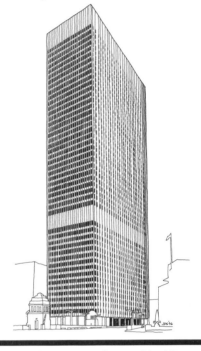

The IBM Building was the last project designed by Mies van der Rohe, one of this century's most influential architects. Born in Germany and named Director of the progressive Bauhaus School in 1930, he left the country amid increasing political unrest and, recruited by John Holabird of the Chicago architectural firm Holabird and Root, in 1938 became Director of Architecture at Chicago's Armour (later Illinois) Institute of Technology. Mies believed that the twentieth century required a new architecture using modern materials and simplified forms. The 52-story IBM Building exemplifies characteristics of his best works: harmonious proportions, elegant materials, and the expression of the building's underlying form through steel and glass. Here, the steel frame and ample 30- by 40-foot bay modules are directly expressed on the exterior's curtain wall of aluminum and double-glazed tinted glass. Placement on the narrow K-shaped site had to accommodate existing train tracks and Chicago Sun-Times storage facilities while providing view corridors to Lake Michigan—constraints that restricted public access to the river's edge. Nonetheless, the IBM Building remains a cool, contained punctuation mark to the 1920s decorative designs along Wacker Drive and the Michigan Avenue Bridge.

Bertrand Goldberg Associates
300 North State Street, between State and Dearborn Streets
1964–7

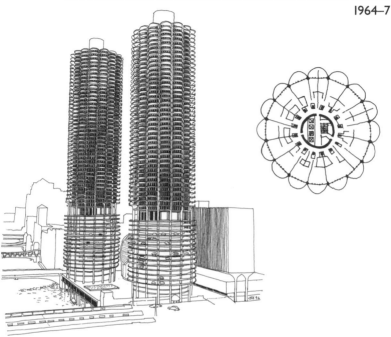

Marina City is noteworthy for its consideration of urban issues as well as for its innovative engineering and design. Commissioned by the International Union of Janitors, architect Bertrand Goldberg (b. 1913) sought to provide attractive, affordable housing in downtown Chicago while incorporating the Chicago River, then a neglected resource, into his design. This "city within a city" originally comprised 900 apartment units in two towers, an office building, restaurants, a theater, and recreational facilities for its residents. Goldberg's recognition of the river as an amenity can be seen in the building's marina, which allows residents to take advantage of their riverfront location. When completed in 1967, the reinforced concrete towers were the tallest in the world; their curving shell forms are functional in their reduction of wind shear, and aesthetic in their exploration of the sculptural possibilities of the material. The method of construction was especially inventive. Because a concrete core, where utilities are located, was built first, the concrete floors could then be poured and attached sequentially in a process that was both time- and cost-efficient. Note the repetition of cantilevered apartment balconies, which creates a distinctive scalloped silhouette.

Quaker Tower
Skidmore, Owings & Merrill
321 North Clark Street
1983–7

Hotel Nikko Chicago
Hellmuth, Obata & Kassabaum
320 North Dearborn Street
1985–7

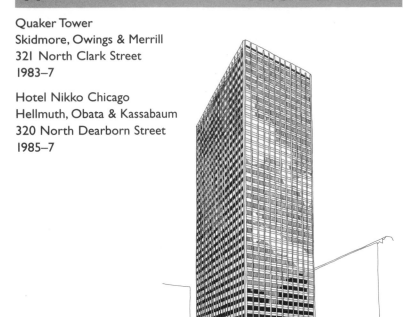

Part of an ensemble fronting the Chicago River that also includes the adjacent Hotel Nikko, Quaker Tower is a 35-story metal and glass flat-roofed tower containing one million square feet of office space. Designed by Bruce Graham in association with studio heads Diane Legge and Richard Tomlinson, Quaker Tower's understated elegance results from the use of blue-green glass to reflect the river's color and a grid of rounded exterior stainless steel mullions that sparkle in the sunlight. A block-long pedestrian promenade connects the tower with the hotel and also provides public access to the river. This walkway is landscaped with continuous rows of upright yews fronted by spreading junipers, creating an inviting, green oasis. A mezzanine level has outdoor seating for the Quaker Oats Company employee cafeteria. At the corner of Clark Street and the river, a small building housing the elevator to the riverwalk mimics the nearby bridge houses, creating a further connection to the riverfront. Directly across the river, Japanese architect Kenzo Tange (b. 1925) designed a riverfront park modeled on the Ryoan-ji Temple garden in Kyoto as a view for Hotel Nikko guests.

George C. Nimmons
325 North LaSalle Street
1913–4
Formerly Reid, Murdoch, and Company

Built for the Reid, Murdoch, and Company wholesale food operation, this building is one of the last remaining warehouse structures along the main branch of the Chicago River and was adaptively reused for City of Chicago offices in 1955. Reflecting its steel and concrete frame, the red brick exterior is a simple rectangular grid, which is enlivened by dark red terra-cotta details, including a lion's head emblematic of the company's Monarch brand name. The riverfront facade balances the horizontality of the building itself with the vertical thrust of a three-story clocktower. The building was once symmetrical; however, one 20-foot bay was removed in 1926 when LaSalle Street was widened in preparation for its new bridge. On the building's north side there were originally 40- by 240-foot freight train sheds for two sets of railroad tracks. On the river side were docking facilities, and the pedestrian promenade still extends along the Chicago River at street level. The building's architect, George Nimmons (1865–1947), was associated with the Prairie School of architecture; in 1904, he and William K. Fellows (1870–1948) co-designed the Sears Roebuck & Company complex on West Arthington Street at Homan Avenue—at the time, the largest Chicago building commission ever received.

13 LaSalle Street Bridge and Bridge Houses

Edward H. Bennett, architect; Thomas G. Pihlfeldt, engineer of bridges; Donald N. Becker, engineer of bridge design
LaSalle Street and the Chicago River
1927–8

This trunnion bascule bridge at LaSalle Street, 86 feet wide and 242 feet across, is second only to the Michigan Avenue Bridge in scale and grandeur. Since the 1909 Plan of Chicago recommended widening LaSalle Street to better organize downtown traffic circulation, the LaSalle Street Bridge received monumental treatment. Planning began in 1914–5, but lack of funding, local protests, and the onset of World War I delayed construction until 1927. At that time, the southern end of Wacker Drive had just been completed (1924–6) and the widening of LaSalle Street at the north end—which resulted in the Central Office Building (see #12) losing a bay—coincided with the commencement of bridge construction. Like the adjacent Clark Street Bridge, built one year later, the LaSalle Street Bridge is supported by pony trusses that provide graceful curved silhouettes where the bridge meets the riverbank. These low trusses do not interfere with sightlines and have no overhead bracing. Heavily ornamented bridge houses designed by architect Edward Bennett distinguish the LaSalle Street Bridge and emphasize its importance. Made of Bedford limestone, they are taller and more detailed than most, with mansard roofs, cartouches, swags, and rusticated masonry.

Helene Curtis Industries Headquarters 14

325 North Wells Street
1914
Adaptive reuse: Booth/Hansen & Associates, 1985
Formerly the Chase & Sanborn
Coffee warehouse

The Helene Curtis Industries Corporate Headquarters is a fine example of adaptive reuse; architect Laurence Booth (b. 1936) transformed a small, neglected coffee warehouse into a corporate headquarters. On the exterior, the facade was kept intact with the addition of a curved green glass rooftop penthouse, which serves as the corporate board room. Its rounded center recalls a ship's prow, an appropriate reference for the Chicago River, once one of the busiest waterways in the world. The river eliminates the need for cooling towers on the roof: river water is circulated through coils in the basement as part of the air-conditioning system. The new building's interior space is organized around the 18- by 20-foot column spacing. Workstations are grouped around these columns, which also function as monumental lighting fixtures. In the lobby the pale green marble floor, walls, and seating add distinction and color. Since the owner markets hair-care products, an actual beauty salon was installed in the lobby overlooking the Chicago River, giving visitors an immediate demonstration of the company's wares. At the lower level facing the river are a cafeteria and a riverfront terrace for employee use.

Graham, Anderson, Probst and White

Merchandise Mart Plaza, north bank of the Chicago River between Wells and Orleans Streets

1923–31

The massive Merchandise Mart, comprising nearly four million square feet, was the largest building in the world until the completion of the Pentagon near Washington, D.C. The Merchandise Mart's five-acre site along the main channel of the Chicago River near the junction of its north and south branches gives it exceptional visual prominence from three directions. The 1909 Plan of Chicago encouraged riverfront development, and Marshall Field and Company decided to consolidate the company's wholesale operations here. Soon space was leased to other distributors as well. Built over the NorthWestern train tracks, the Merchandise Mart is among Chicago's first air rights developments and was expected to be part of a new business district north of the river until the Great Depression intervened. Framed in steel and sheathed in buff Bedford limestone, its large mass is articulated by a series of horizontal cornice lines, a central shaft and tower, corner bays capped with turrets, and green and gold accents. The lobby is decorated with murals by Jules Guerin, who also illustrated the 1909 Plan of Chicago. Enhanced by its recent cleaning and renovation, its site, scale, and stylized details create a powerful presence on the Chicago River.

Warehouse: Schmidt, Garden and Martin
Merchandise building: Company in-house design staff
Tower: Minoru Yamasaki
618 West Chicago Avenue and the north
branch of the Chicago River
Warehouse, 1906–8;
merchandise building, 1929;
tower, 1974

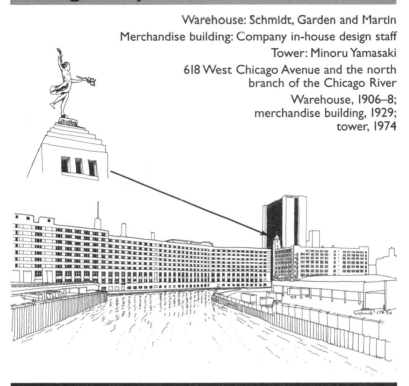

Snaking along the north branch of the Chicago River, this cream-colored, nine-story trapezoidal mass averaging 800 by 200 feet was the largest reinforced concrete building of its time when it was completed in 1908. It was the second Montgomery Ward Company commission for Richard Schmidt (1865–1958), who had previously designed the company's new office tower (see Michigan Avenue #14). This warehouse complex, which consolidated all company operations, was located along the Chicago River to take advantage of both rail and water transport for the distribution of mail-order goods. It follows the river edge with sleek horizontal lines interspersed with stylized, decorative motifs common to the Prairie School of architecture. This style is known for its use of long, low lines and geometric patterns, suggesting the flat vistas of the midwestern prairie, and can be seen in Frank Lloyd Wright's concurrent work. Schmidt was born in Germany but came to Chicago a year later; he studied architecture at the Massachusetts Institute of Technology. In 1906 Schmidt and fellow architect Hugh Garden (1873–1961) designed the elegant Madlener House, home of the Graham Foundation for Advanced Studies in the Fine Arts. They later formed a successful partnership with architect Edgar Martin (1871–1951).

Harry Weese and Associates
357–65 North Canal Street
1990

These four River Cottages facing the Chicago River are located at the foot of the Kinzie Street Bridge, the terminus of Chicago's first railroad line, the Galena and Chicago Union. In November 1848, the first grain transported by rail arrived at this site, where it was loaded onto ships for transport to eastern markets. Smaller boats, owned by residents, now moor at the River Cottages. These five- and six-level townhouses have units ranging from 2,200 to 4,200 square feet. An internal elevator and stairs connect the various living levels. The stucco townhouses have tubular steel frames and concrete deck floors. Their articulated cross-bracing and angular profile are reminiscent of the historic schooner sails and riggings familiar to architect Harry Weese (b. 1915), an accomplished sailor. Weese, who received his architectural training at the Massachusetts Institute of Technology and Cranbrook Academy, has devoted much of his career to the planning, preservation, and improvement of the Chicago riverfront. In this imaginative design, portholes, decks, and balconies all reference the river. Such small-scale development is rare along valuable waterfront property and makes a special contribution to the cityscape.

Frank Abbott
345 North Canal Street
1908
Adaptive reuse: Harry Weese and Associates, 1979–81
Formerly American Cold
Storage Warehouse

Standing between the train tracks and the Chicago River, the sixteen-story pink brick American Cold Storage Warehouse was among Chicago's first steel and concrete buildings. Architect Harry Weese faced several problems when he began to renovate the structure in 1979 for residential condominium use. First of all, the original building had been constructed in two phases, each with its own structural system—one of poured-in-place reinforced concrete spanning steel beams, the other with vaulted lightweight aggregate floors. Weese rebuilt these sections where necessary to form an integrated frame. Next, the architect had to create 500 windows for the planned living units, which required punching through exterior masonry walls twelve to sixteen inches thick without damaging their structural integrity. He met this challenge by devising a system that allowed the walls to be cut through from both sides. This adaptive reuse project, successfully completed in 1981, created 104 loft-style condominiums, including top floor duplexes, and 20,000 square feet of commercial space at the building's base. Renamed Fulton House, it provides superb views and accessibility to Chicago's Loop, while offering residents boat moorings and a waterside deck.

Perkins & Will
100 North Riverside Plaza, between Randolph and Washington Streets
1988–90

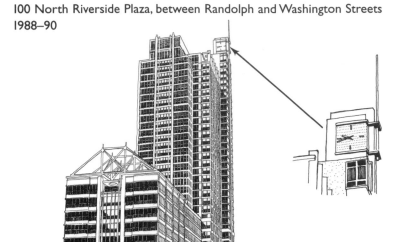

The 36-story, mixed-use Morton International Building presented several challenges to architect Ralph Johnson (b. 1948) and his project team. It was a particularly difficult site—long, narrow, irregular, and bounded by the Chicago River on the east. Furthermore, the passage through this site by the busy Metra commuter railroad line added the complication of building over existing tracks and rights-of-way. Johnson's design differentiates the various building uses as simple rectilinear blocks with geometric patterns on the gray granite, glass, and metal exterior. These blocks are then connected by a pedestrian arcade of 15-foot repeating columns and by a clocktower placed asymmetrically toward the northern end of the building. This clocktower is a public amenity in itself and recalls others along the riverfront at the Central Office Building (see #12) and the Wrigley Building (see #8). Since a structural column could not be placed where the train tracks curved, a rooftop truss was used to redistribute loads. This exposed form reflects the structure of nearby Chicago River bridges. In order to ensure public access to the riverfront, a linear park at the river's edge was retained, with stairways leading to it from the street level.

Holabird and Root
400 West Madison Street
1925–9
Formerly Chicago Daily News Building

Headquarters for the old Chicago Daily News during its heyday, this was the first building in Chicago to use the air rights above railroad tracks and it pioneered development across the Chicago River west of the Loop. Initial framing problems were solved by using large double 12-foot girders to cantilever parts of the building over the tracks. Placed parallel to the Chicago River at the western edge of its block-long site, the 26-story limestone building is intersected by a series of piers at its base that are repeated on a grander scale at the edges and sides of the building. Its flat central slab is punctuated by slightly recessed rectangular windows. Alvin Meyer's bas-reliefs depict the history of printing at ground level and a two-story covered concourse connects Riverside Plaza to the Northwestern Atrium (see #21). The plaza's pedestrian walkway along the river was the site of nightly band concerts in the 1930s. A fine example of the 1920s style called Art Moderne (or Art Deco when highly decorated), the building's bold design and innovative engineering won gold medals in 1930 from both the Architectural League of New York and the American Institute of Architects.

Murphy/Jahn
500 West Madison Street
1979–87

The Northwestern Atrium, which replaced the Beaux Arts masonry Chicago and North Western Terminal designed by Frost and Granger in 1911, is a 37-story, 1.6-million-square-foot glass and aluminum complex. The new building evokes the spatial grandeur of nineteenth-century train stations while dealing with the challenge of multi-use space and levels. Both commuters and tenants enter a 90-foot-high skylit retail gallery that extends the entire length of the facade. Ground-level escalators lead to a 110-foot-high atrium at train level; a second escalator bank leads to the office lobby above. On the exterior, dark-blue enameled aluminum ribbons emphasize the building's verticality; the Art Deco style is suggested by the streamlined horizontal glass curves cascading down the tripartite facade, with its central rounded tower. Note also how the building's Madison Street silhouette echoes that of Riverside Plaza, which was completed in 1929. Northwestern Atrium's concentric arched entry recalls those of Chicago's demolished Transportation and Stock Exchange Buildings, both designed by noted architect Louis Sullivan in the late nineteenth century. This complex is a fine example of architect Helmut Jahn's work, which integrates curving, muscular, colorful forms with structural expressiveness.

Gateway I–IV and MidAmerica Commodity Exchange
Skidmore, Owings & Merrill
100–300 South Riverside Plaza
1963–83

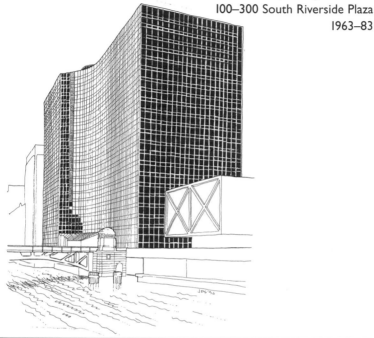

Gateway Center is a five-building project built along the west bank of the Chicago River over railroad tracks that lead to Union Station. All of the Gateway Center buildings except Gateway IV were designed by Bruce Graham. Gateways I and II are identical twenty-story glass and black steel office towers that echo the historic twin brick Butler Brothers Warehouses along the Chicago River to the north, built by the office of Daniel Burnham in 1913 and 1922. Gateway III is a 35-story steel frame office building. Next to it is the five-story MidAmerica Commodity Exchange, marked by exposed X-braces and cantilevered over the commuter entrance to Union Station. In the mid-1980s, the pedestrian plaza along the Chicago River connecting these buildings was improved with additional landscaping and public amenities. Gateway IV, the last and largest building of the group, was designed by James DeStefano (b. 1938). Its 22 stories contain over one million square feet of office space. The curving facade of reflective glass complements a bend in the Chicago River and contrasts with the rigid rectangles of the other four Gateway Center buildings. Note the commuter train activity visible at the lower level.

Bertrand Goldberg Associates
800 South Wells Street
Phase I, 1984–6

The serpentine concrete curves of River City hug the Chicago River just south of the Loop. This complex, ten to seventeen stories high, contains 446 apartments, retail and commercial space and a health club. Built on land previously owned by the Baltimore and Ohio Railroad, the project was originally intended to be four 85-story towers linked by skywalks, but the City of Chicago approved a lower scale and density for the site. River City expresses architect Bertrand Goldberg's continuing interest in designing urban complexes that combine affordable housing with working and recreational amenities, as evidenced in his earlier Marina City project (see #10). A native of Chicago, Goldberg trained at Harvard University and at the Bauhaus in Germany under Mies van der Rohe. Other well-known Chicago buildings by Goldberg include the Raymond Hilliard Center (1966) and Northwestern University's Prentice Women's Hospital and Maternity Center (1974–5). His work is informed by his commitment to using architecture to help solve urban issues, his use of concrete as an expressive sculptural material, and his pioneering regard for the Chicago riverfront.

Kohn Pedersen Fox
Associate Architects: Harwood K. Smith
and Partners
1990

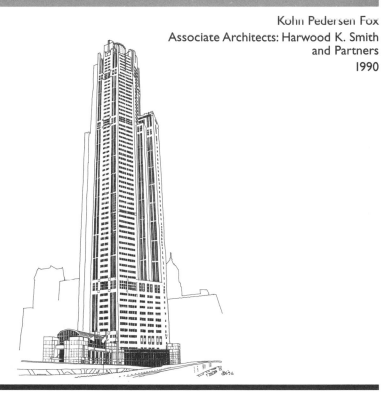

Standing in the shadow of the legendary Sears Tower, this 65-story, 1.4-million-square-foot building is the tallest reinforced concrete structure in the world. One of three towers planned for this block-long site facing South Wacker Drive, 311 South Wacker Drive is distinguished by red/pink granite cladding and, at night, by the brightly lit glass cylinder crowning its tower. The building is centered around a "winter garden," a glass vaulted area intended to act as a hub for the complex that includes giant palm trees, a waterfall, and a restaurant. The massing of the building explores a variety of geometric configurations: the octagonal tower above the fifty-first floor rises from a rectangular midsection that in turn is grounded in an irregularly shaped base. To bind together the elements of the design, architect William Pedersen (b. 1938) repeated the horizontal banding at the base of the thirteenth and forty-sixth floors. Pedersen's firm, Kohn Pedersen Fox, founded in 1976 in New York City, has designed several large buildings in Chicago during the 1980s (see #29 and #30 and Michigan Avenue #42).

Skidmore, Owings & Merrill
233 South Wacker Drive
1968–74; entrance addition, 1984–5
Renovation: DeStefano + Partners, 1992–3

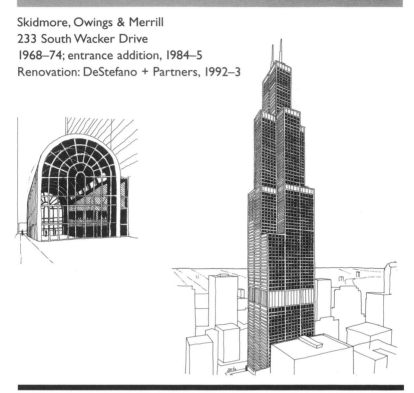

At 110 stories and 1,454 feet high, the Sears Tower is among the tallest buildings in the world. To ensure stability, a system of 75-foot-square structural tubes is used, to act as perimeter columns to brace the skyscraper against powerful wind forces. Nine of these huge tubes form the building's base. As the building rises, the number of tubes is reduced where setbacks occur: at the fiftieth, sixty-sixth, and ninetieth floors. Two tubes remain to support the tower, while steel columns comprising the building's frame serve to channel wind shear and gravity stress down to bedrock caissons. Design partner Bruce Graham (b. 1925) and engineer Fazlur Khan (1929–82) led the project team for this immense undertaking. It both symbolized Sears Roebuck and Company's position as the largest retailer in the world and consolidated the company's offices. With its dark angular silhouette, the Sears Tower soon became a Chicago icon, but it was forbidding at street level. Several years ago, Skidmore, Owings & Merrill returned to design a vaulted atrium as a friendlier entrance and to renovate the lobby. Recent work by DeStefano + Partners has created a more inviting lobby and better tourist access.

Harry Weese and Associates
1979–81

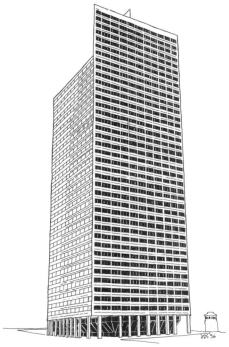

This 38-story, 850,000-square-foot office tower is situated on a small, irregular site, yet architect Harry Weese's design maximizes both floor size and riverside location. Weese's fascination with the triangular form, seen in other Chicago works, such as the Swissôtel in Illinois Center (see #40) and the River Cottages (see #17), is also evident here: the asymmetrical four-sided polygon is composed of two right triangles sharing a hypotenuse. The triangles' differing heights—one rises seven stories above the other— reveal the geometric configuration. A special feature of the building is its three-story glass-enclosed lobby facing the Chicago River that fills the interior with natural light. This emphasis on light is also evident in the building's exterior: white painted aluminum panels alternating with reflective glass give the building a bright sparkling facade among its darker high-rise neighbors. In 1988, Harry Weese designed Quincy Park, adjacent to the tower at the river's edge. This pocket park was donated by developers John Buck, Wes Irvine, and JMB/Urban and modeled on Manhattan's Paley Park. The park's summertime seating, greenery, and waterfall make it a special riverfront amenity.

Fujikawa Johnson and Associates
10 and 30 South Wacker Drive
1983–7

This carnelian granite complex comprises two 1.1-million-square-foot office towers flanking the ten-story Chicago Mercantile Exchange. Beneath its smooth exterior and simple massing are sophisticated solutions to several engineering and design challenges. Since the Exchange required a 40,000-square-foot space with no supporting columns to provide maximum visibility for trading activity, engineers used 140- by 35-foot trusses to support the ceiling, then redistributed this weight to a thickened wall system and wide perimeter columns. These walls would have caused the towers to tilt under their own weight, so the towers were built slightly bowed; as they were occupied, the curves corrected themselves until the towers became properly aligned. Since the site measured 17,000 square feet less than the building program requirements, additional leasing space was provided by cantilevering both towers 32 feet over the Mercantile Exchange. Finally, financial prudence mandated constructing the second tower only after the first was leased, while keeping the Exchange operations undisturbed. Thus, the towers, although identical, had to be independently configured and engineered. The towers have separate entrances, and distinctive serrated corners create sixteen window offices per floor.

Graham, Anderson, Probst and White
20 North Wacker Drive
1927–9

Designed by Alfred Shaw (1895–1970) for Graham, Anderson, Probst, and White, the Civic Opera Building is a complex structure housing an auditorium for the Opera House, the smaller Civic Theatre, and in the middle, a 45-story office building. Samuel Insull (1859–1938), a utilities magnate, and fellow opera subscribers financed the construction of the $20 million building with the intention that office rents would support the cost of opera operations. Unfortunately, the building opened just after the 1929 stock market crash and soon both Insull and the opera were bankrupt. The Civic Opera Building is located by the river, in a former warehouse district at the western edge of the Loop, an area that was redeveloped in the 1920s. It fronts on Wacker Drive with a block-long, seventeen-bay colonnade connecting the auditorium spaces at each end; these entrances are marked by arched pediments containing sculptured bas-reliefs. Decorative details on the facade, including garlands, comedy and tragedy masks, putti, and lyres, represent music and the performing arts. Jules Guerin, also known for his watercolors of Burnham's Plan of Chicago and for the Merchandise Mart murals (see #15), was responsible for the interior design.

Kohn Pedersen Fox with Perkins & Will
1979–83

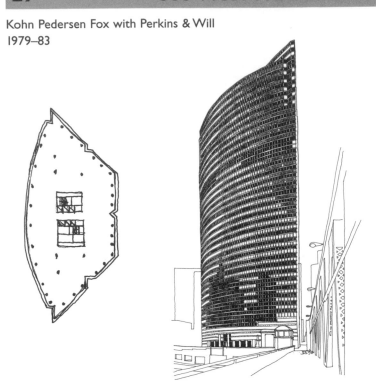

The building at 333 West Wacker Drive is a curving green glass wedge located where the Chicago River divides into its north and south branches. At this triangular site, the grid of the city meets the river bend, and the plan of this 36-story, 850,155-square-foot building is shaped by the transition between the two environments. On the Loop side, the building follows the street edges to form a truncated triangle, while above the Franklin Street entrance a notch in the glass facade creates acute angles that give a prismatic quality to the building surface. Blessed by uninterrupted view corridors, the building's river facade is a taut arc that reflects clouds, shadows, and silhouetted shapes. Internationally acclaimed and locally appreciated, sensitive to both a gentle waterway and an urban bustle, 333 West Wacker Drive is a spectacular addition to Chicago's riverfront. The three-story monumental base of polished granite and Vermont marble with a pedestrian arcade raises the office floors above the elevated train tracks at the rear of the building. Louvered medallions hide mechanical vents, becoming decorative elements in themselves and providing a visual link to the adjacent building to the east, also designed by William Pedersen.

Kohn Pedersen Fox with Perkins & Will
1985–9

This 31-story, 644,167-square-foot granite and glass skyscraper provides a striking contrast to the curved green glass tower next door at 333 West Wacker Drive, which was designed by the same architect, William Pederson, a few years earlier. Known as a "contextual architect," Pedersen designs buildings that fit their urban setting by referencing existing street patterns, forms, materials, and structures. For instance, 225 West Wacker Drive was the last site in the grid of the city facing the Chicago River until the river curves to form its south branch—hence the choice of masonry cladding and rectangular form typical of downtown Chicago buildings. The four spires recall the Merchandise Mart's corner towers directly across the river and are tied together by metal elements that reference the Chicago River's bridges. Although different in materials, shape, and size, 225 and 333 West Wacker Drive are linked by the repetition of common forms, such as their circular louvered vents, as well as by the shared horizontal street line formed by the three-story lobbies.

Graham, Anderson, Probst and White
1927
Renovation and addition: Skidmore, Owings, & Merrill, 1980–6
Formerly Builders Building

Planned as an office, distribution, and exhibition center for the construction trades and associated merchants, the Builders Building symbolizes Chicago's building boom of the 1920s. Note the row of three-story columns just below the cornice line of the original 1927 building that add an element of grandeur to an otherwise foursquare mass of glazed brick and terra cotta. In 1980, since the adjoining property was too small for a separate building, the developer decided to add to the existing structure. The sympathetic design of architect Adrian Smith (see #4) doubled the size of the original building, yet matched its scale, proportions, and color; a sloping four-story glass penthouse unifies the composition visually. The addition's bay windows repeat the rhythm of the original building's windows but create wider views of the river and perhaps inspired those of the Hotel Nikko Chicago just across the river. As part of the restoration, marble, terra cotta, and cast-iron pieces were carefully matched or replicated. The LaSalle Street lobby was completely redesigned and is now a splendid four-story-high space, complete with a skylight that had been hidden for years.

Holabird and Root with Rebori, Wentworth, Dewey, and McCormick
221 North LaSalle Street
1929–30

Located at the head of the LaSalle Street financial district, the 41-story lime-stone and granite LaSalle-Wacker Building was developed by two wealthy Chicagoans, cousins Joseph Medill Patterson and Robert McCormick, for tenants associated with the banking industry. Two firms collaborated on the building; it is unclear which served as principal designer. While the building's bold, simplified setback form reflects Holabird and Roche's style, most scholars attribute it to Andrew Rebori (1886–1966), based on his close associations with the McCormick family. Rebori was a talented, idiosyn-cratic architect whose best work exhibits an originality that challenges styl-istic classification. He organized the LaSalle-Wacker Building on an H-shaped plan, with an indented central portion rising above the first 24 stories to become a wide, freestanding tower. This center setback gives the building its thronelike appearance and functions as a light well for the surrounding offices. Like several notable buildings designed during the 1920s, such as the Wrigley Building (#8) and the Tribune Tower and Printing Plant (#5), the LaSalle-Wacker Building included a lighting pro-gram—in this case a powerful rooftop beacon that showed its setbacks to an advantage.

DeStefano and Partners
Design Consultants: Taller de Arquitectura
77 West Wacker Drive
1992

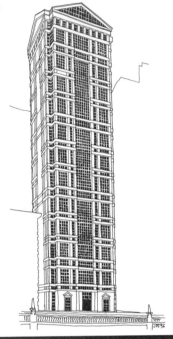

Clad in white Portuguese Royal granite with a silver-gray curtain wall, this 50-story building reinterprets classical forms on a monumental scale. Decorative details are simplified; the enormous pediments that crown each facade are the building's most striking feature. Smaller gables are repeated on the doorways that punctuate the tower's 42-foot-high base. The gridded glass shaft is divided into sections by double horizontal stone bands and has notched edges that create eight corner offices per floor to take advantage of the spectacular vistas enhanced by the Chicago River's view corridor. The building lobby is designed as a museum space with sculpture and paintings by noted contemporary artists. Consulting architect Ricardo Bofill (b. 1939), who founded the Taller de Arquitectura (Architectural Workshop) in 1963 in Barcelona, Spain, is an internationally recognized modern classicist known for his inventive use of superscaled architectural elements, such as arches and columns. Other examples of his work include the Rice University School of Music in Houston, Texas, several housing projects in Spain, and the development of three new towns near Paris, France. This high-rise is his first project in Chicago.

Kevin Roche–John Dinkeloo and Associates
35 West Wacker Drive
1989

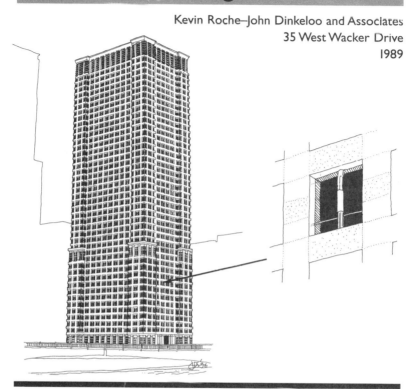

This 50-story building, with its masonry cladding, flat top, and solid shaft, projects a solid, conservative image for its major tenant, the Leo Burnett Company, Chicago's largest advertising agency. Irish-born architect Kevin Roche (b. 1922) trained at the Illinois Institute of Technology before joining Eero Saarinen's firm, which became Kevin Roche–John Dinkeloo and Associates upon Saarinen's death in 1961. The firm is well known for its corporate and museum work, and Roche himself received the prestigious Pritzker Prize in Architecture in 1982. This building, his first Chicago commission, reflects a concern for maintaining the street wall and cornice lines of existing buildings along Wacker Drive. On this highly visible site facing the Chicago River, Roche designed a skyscraper conforming to Louis Sullivan's classic definition: a clearly defined base, shaft, and capital. The building is also placed within the Chicago architectural tradition by Roche's inventive reinterpretation of the Chicago window. Here, the windows are recessed within stainless steel reveals and divided in half vertically by polished stainless steel mullions. These bars catch available light, creating a variable, sparkling surface pattern that animates the dark facade.

Thielbar and Fugard with Giaver and Dinkleberg
35 East Wacker Drive
1924–6
Later Pure Oil Building,
now known by its address

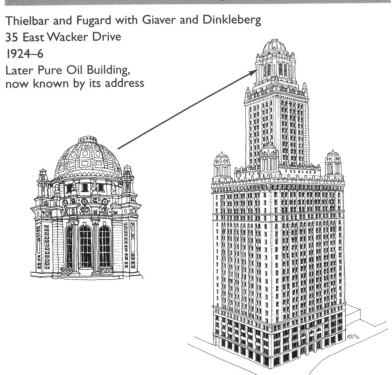

Based on the fifteenth-century chapel for the Certosa of Pavia, an Italian monastery noted for its harmonious detail, the Jewelers Building is clad in highly decorative terra-cotta tiles. Perhaps this surface ornamentation appealed to the jewelry designers, wholesalers, and retailers for whom this building was designed. Its massing, however, is simpler than its surface: a 17-story tower rises from a 24-story base and is capped with a belvedere offering panoramic views of the city to its fortunate tenant. At the twenty-fourth floor was a roof promenade and at the base of the tower was once an open-air terrace. Since the building was surrounded by public streets, adequate natural light was available without a light well, so the developers provided a parking garage in the central core, which appealed to security-conscious jewelers. Entering from lower Wacker Drive, automobiles and drivers were delivered by elevator to their parking or office floor. By 1940, mechanical problems made the garage impractical and it was converted to office space. Architects Frederick J. Thielbar (1866–1941) and John Reed Fugard (1886–1968) became partners in 1925 and designed several other buildings in Chicago. Associated architect Frederick P. Dinkelberg (c. 1869–1935) had previously worked in Daniel Burnham's office.

Harry Weese and Associates
55 East Wacker Drive
1968

In 1879, Mary Baker Eddy (1821–1910), who based her teachings on the healing methods of Jesus, organized the First Church of Christ, Scientist in Boston, Massachusetts. As the Christian Science faith flourished, additional churches were built, many of distinctive design; this Seventeenth Church of Christ, Scientist fits that tradition. Given a prominent angled site, architect Harry Weese (b. 1915) used the semi-circular auditorium space to define the low, curving exterior from which rises a lead-coated, conical roof crowned with a domed lantern. The auditorium features a sound-diffusing ceiling and has 925 seats encircling the reader's platform. The church is isolated from street traffic by a lobby and has a sunken garden that admits natural light to the Sunday School one level below grade. Long horizontal windows at the base of the roof and the dome provide additional light to the auditorium. The entire facade, including the steel girders supporting the roof, is sheathed in travertine marble. Directly east is a seven-story triangular building that houses church offices, meeting rooms, mechanical systems, and other related facilities. A peaceful oasis in the middle of the city's bustle, this church is an expressive contrast to the office towers that surround it.

Herbert Hugh Riddle
75 East Wacker Drive
1926–8
Renovation: Harry Weese and Associates, 1982–3
Later Lincoln Tower,
now known by its address

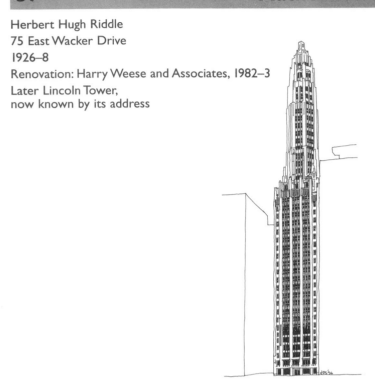

This slender, white, 42-story terra-cotta tower with a lantern crown evolved from the same eclectic decorative idiom and materials as the near-by Wrigley Building, which was designed a few years earlier. Initially, owner Alonzo Mather planned twin towers (the second, at 324–30 North Michigan Avenue) that would be joined by a ground floor arcade and topped with a radio antenna. However, after the 1929 stock market crash, plans for the second tower were abandoned. Facing Wacker Drive and the Chicago River, the building is a 24-story shaft with setbacks to the rear at the ninth and sixteenth floors. The octagonal tower is set back in a series of recesses, with one tenant per floor, until the top two levels measure only 350 and 280 square feet, respectively. Designed by Herbert Hugh Riddle (1875–1939), architect of the Chicago Theological Seminary, and built at a cost of $2,617,040, Mather Tower was renovated by Harry Weese and Associates in 1983. Alonzo Mather, a descendent New England preacher Cotton Mather, invented the Mather Stock Car for the humane transport of livestock; he is said to have been responsible for several of the building's design features, including its octagonal tower.

Alfred S. Alschuler
360 North Michigan Avenue
1922–3

As the Wrigley Building (see #8) was nearing completion, Alfred Alschuler (1876–1940) received a plum commission: the headquarters building for the London Guarantee & Accident Company, which would occupy the prominent site just across the Chicago River at the termination of Wacker Drive with the new Michigan Avenue Bridge. Alschuler was known primarily for his industrial work, although he also designed the terra-cotta Thompson Building (1912) at 350 North Clark Street, the K. A. M. Isaiah-Israel Synagogue in Chicago's Kenwood neighborhood, and the old Chicago Mercantile Exchange (1927) at 110 North Franklin Street. Here, on the historic site of Fort Dearborn, he designed a 22-story Indiana limestone building using classical references throughout, from the three-story columns marking the entrance, repeated above the fifteenth floor, to the Greco-Roman tempietto on top. This aesthetic is consistent with Burnham's 1909 Plan of Chicago, which envisioned the development of the riverfront in the grand Beaux Arts tradition. Note how the rusticated base matches that of the Wacker Drive Esplanade below and how the unusual concave facade accommodates the semicircular plaza defining the intersection of Michigan Avenue with Wacker Drive.

Holabird and Root
1927–8

The last-built of the four original buildings located at the Michigan Avenue Bridge, 333 North Michigan Avenue resembles a slender gatepost when seen from the length of North Michigan Avenue. Clad in granite and limestone, its design reflects the sleek, Art Deco aesthetic of its time: the mass of the eleven-story tower rising from the 24-story main block is modified by a series of setbacks that emphasize its verticality, as does the absence of a cornice. At the fifth floor of the building are a series of seven-foot-high bas-reliefs by sculptor Fred M. Torrey, depicting the growth and early history of Chicago: The Portage, the Hunter, Pioneer Women, the Attack on Fort Dearborn, the Covered Wagon Era, and the Traders. These reliefs harmonize with the overall massing of the building in their bold, simplified lines; they also typify the interest of the era in incorporating sculptural design into the architectural program. Holabird and Root, formed in 1928, was the successor firm to Holabird and Roche and continues to practice today. Its notable designs include the Palmolive Building (see Michigan Avenue #41), the Chicago Daily News Building (1925–9) (see #20), and the Board of Trade (1929–30) (see Loop, #8).

Office of and successor firms to Mies van der Rohe, with other firms
Bounded by East Wacker Drive, Lake Michigan, East Lake Street, and
Michigan Avenue
Begun in 1967

Illinois Center is an 83-acre development on the site of former railyards; it is planned to ultimately comprise 16 million square feet of office space, 7,500 residential units, and 3,500 hotel rooms. Since Illinois Center has a triple-decked street system east of Michigan Avenue, building entrances are high above the ground and separated from the riverfront. Pedestrian movement is primarily via an interior concourse linking buildings in the area. In the 1920s, when the land first became available for development, such notable architects as Holabird and Root and Eliel Saarinen planned dense developments. However, construction did not begin until 1967, when Mies van der Rohe designed One Illinois Center, a 30-story black glass and steel office tower. After Mies' death in 1969, his successor firm, Fujikawa, Conterato, Lohan and Associates, continued as architects, designing office towers Two and Three Illinois Center as well as Boulevard Towers. Hotel and apartment projects built more recently have added variety by using different forms and cladding materials. For example, the Swissôtel, designed by Harry Weese and Associates, is a shiny aluminum triangle. Although pedestrian amenities have been added recently, Illinois Center would benefit greatly from more green spaces and riveredge uses.

Glossary

acroteria. A pedestal at the corners and peak of a roof to support a statue or ornament; more usually, the ornament itself.

antefix(ae). A decorated upright slab used in classical architecture to close or conceal the open end of a row of tilies that cover the joints of roof tiles.

arcade. A series of arches supported by columns or piers; a building or part of a building with a series of arches.

architrave. The ornamental moldings around the faces of the jambs and lintel of a doorway or window.

bas-relief. A carving, embossing, or casting moderately protruding from the background plane, from the French meaning "low-relief."

bearing wall. A wall that carries a portion of a building's weight.

belvedere. A rooftop pavilion from which a vista can be enjoyed, from the Italian meaning "beautiful view."

bifora. A double-arched opening within a larger arched frame.

brace. A metal or wood member, which may be curved (portal) or straight (knee), and is used to stiffen or support a structure.

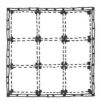

bundled tube. A structural system consisting of closely spaced columns tied together for strength, which, used at a building's outer wall, act as the walls of a hollow tube. The Sears Tower uses this system.

cantilever. A projecting beam or part of a structure that is supported at only one end.

cartouche. An ornamental panel in the form of a scroll, circle, or oval, often bearing an inscription.

cast iron. Smelted iron, shaped in a mold, whose compressive or load-bearing strength made it an important structural metal.

cavetto. A concave surface or molding about a quarter of a circle in section, often used in cornices, especially in Egyptian architecture.

Chicago School of architecture. High-rise commercial buildings designed in Chicago in the late nineteenth century, made possible by elevators and linked by construction similarities, including the use of a metal structural (skeleton) frame to support the building; bay, oriel, or Chicago windows to admit maximum light; and the use of the latest wind-bracing and foundation technologies.

Chicago window. A window flanked at each side by a narrow movable sash and occupying the full width of the bay in which it is placed.

coffering. A ceiling with deeply recessed, often highly ornamented panels.

console. A decorated bracket in the form of a vertical scroll, projecting from a wall to support a cornice, door, or window head.

cornice. A projecting ornamental molding along the top of a building, wall, or arch, finishing or crowning it.

 **crocket.** In Gothic architecture, an upward-oriented ornament, often vegetal in form, regularly spaced along sloping or vertical edges of spires, pinnacles, or gables.

esplanade. A level open space for walking or driving, often providing a view.

flying buttress. A bar of masonry, usually sloping, carried on an arch, abutting a solid pier sufficient to receive the thrust of a roof or vault. A characteristic feature of Gothic construction.

footprint. The outline of a building at the ground.

light well. An open area in the center of a building used to provide natural light and ventilation, before the widespread use of electricity and air-conditioning, for the rooms or offices contained in the surrounding sides of the building.

mullion. A vertical member separating and often supporting windows, doors, or panels set in a series.

ogee. A double curve resembling an S-shape, formed by the union of a convex and a concave line.

oriel. A protruding window.

pediment. In classical architecture, the triangular gable end of a roof above the horizontal cornice; more commonly, the triangular or curved ornament used over doors or windows.

Plan of Chicago. The City of Chicago's first comprehensive planning document, prepared by Daniel Burnham and Edward Bennett, which included the development of efficient transportation systems and waterfront beautification projects. It was informed by such Beaux Arts ideas as grand boulevards, monuments, and other civic improvements.

pony truss. A low support without any overhead bracing. Structural supports are above and below the roadway.

Prairie School of architecture. A midwestern movement that sought to create buildings, chiefly residential, reflecting the flat, horizontal terrain of the Midwest and that used distinctive stylized floral or geometric patterns.

quatrefoil. A four-lobed pattern divided by cusps.

rustication. Masonry cut in rough, massive blocks separated from each other by deep joints.

setback. An architectural element in which the upper stories of a tall building are stepped back from the lower stories to permit more light to reach street level.

skeleton frame. A freestanding structure of iron or steel that supports the weight of a building and on which the floors and outer covering are hung.

soffit. The underside of an architectural element.

spandrel. In a multistory building, a wall panel that fills the space between the top of a window in one story and the sill of the window in the story above.

tempietto. A small temple, especially one of ornamental character, resembling those built during the Renaissance.

terra cotta. Cast and fired clay units, usually more intricately modeled than bricks, used for decorative and/or fireproofing architectural purposes.

trunnion bascule bridge. A span that moves in a vertical plane about a horizontal axis and is supported by an axle or trunnion, a pin or pivot about which it rotates.

 **truss.** A structure composed of a combination of members, often steel or iron, usually in some triangular arrangement so as to form a rigid framework.

Index of Architects

Index of Buildings

(Italics indicate buildings referenced in text.)

Notes

Notes

Notes